"Five hundred years ago, everybody [...]
The lord owned everything, and the steward managed his assets. Today,
believers need to remember that God owns it all and we're His stewards.
More than Money is a great reminder that we're called to manage all of
His stuff for His glory."

—DAVE RAMSEY, *best-selling author and*
nationally syndicated radio show host

"I first read Calvin Partain's book about stewardship many years ago in
its initial printing. Even then, I thought he captured the essence of stewardship in the most concise way I had ever seen. Now, with the updated
information and emphasis on the total aspect of God's intent for us in
terms of what we 'owe' back to Him—I have decided that this version
of the book is the one that should be read by every member of every
finance committee, stewardship committee, personnel committee, missions committee, pastor search committee, well . . . every church member! Stewardship is not just about money and talents. It is about our relationships, our experiences, our pain and the fact that God has entrusted
us with the telling of His story. It truly is about *More than Money*."

—DAVID GEORGE, *president of the WMU Foundation*

"I first met Calvin Partain more than 40 years ago when my husband
Dalton and I were North American missionaries on the Navajo res-
ervation. Our churches were in the same association; he and his wife
Marion frequently surprised us with encouragement in many forms.
Several years later, Brother Calvin was our pastor. Without exception,
every time he preached, I discovered some new thought or truth. 'Some
day I'm going to write a book,' he often said to me. God clearly ordained
this writing assignment for him. Now, with a new title and look, his
book will once again call readers to an enlightening discovery of stewardship. Thank you, Brother Calvin, for being a good steward of all God
has given you."

—DR. JUDITH EDWARDS, *retired North American Mission Board*
missionary and Baptist Convention of New Mexico missions
mobilization team leader, former WMU editor and writer,
and current WMU Foundation trustee

CALVIN T. PARTAIN

MORE THAN MONEY

BEING A STEWARD OF ALL GOD'S GIVEN YOU

NEW HOPE®
PUBLISHERS
Gospel-Centered. Missions-Driven.

BIRMINGHAM, ALABAMA

New Hope® Publishers
PO Box 12065
Birmingham, AL 35202–2065
NewHopePublishers.com
New Hope Publishers is a division of WMU®.

Library of Congress Cataloging-in-Publication Data
Names: Partain, Calvin T., author.
Title: More than Money : Being a steward of all God's given you / Calvin T.
    Partain.
Other titles: Trusted stewardship
Description: Birmingham, AL : New Hope Publishers, 2016. | Revised edition
    of: Trusted stewardship. Birmingham, Ala. : Woman's Missionary Union,
    c1996. | Includes index.
Identifiers: LCCN 2016009395 | ISBN 9781596694743 (sc)
Subjects: LCSH: Christian stewardship.
Classification: LCC BV772 .P35 2016 | DDC 248/.6--dc23
LC record available at http://lccn.loc.gov/2016009395

ISBN-10: 1-59669-474-2
ISBN-13: 978-1-59669-474-3

N164114 • 0616 • 2.5M1

DEDICATION

I dedicate this book to my God-given family who have
fulfilled a vital role in developing my stewardship.

Marion, my wife for 56 years,
is described in Proverbs 31:19–31.

My three children:
David, Walter, and Paula

My five grandchildren:
Elicia, Jared, Michele, Andrew, Jacob

CONTENTS

INTRODUCTION

I write this as an update of my book, *Trusted Steward*, published by Woman's Missionary Union® in 1996, which obviously emphasized being trusted. This book encourages stewards to be faithful according to Jesus' parable of the bags of gold in Matthew 25, which emphasizes both trust and faithfulness.

The subject of stewardship is not new. Often when we hear the word stewardship, it is only in the context of how we use our money, especially in regard to giving to our local church. But stewardship is about more than money. This book is an effort to open the wealth of meanings and blessings that await anyone who decides to become a faithful steward.

My view of the Bible includes 70 years of sincere Bible study and application on life's road. I am thoroughly convinced the Bible is truly God's Word. In 11 years as a trustee of Southeastern Baptist Theological Seminary, I became familiar with the arguments of "scholars" who had varying viewpoints toward God's Word. How do I know the Bible is God's true Word? Simple. When I do what His Word says, I receive what it promises: blessings and/or chastisements. Throughout my life, I am convinced that God has spoken to me through the Bible, and what I believe He has said to me always agrees with the rest of His Word.

This book is an effort to describe the blessings that await anyone who decides to become a faithful steward. I hope and pray you find it helpful on your spiritual journey.

CHAPTER 1

FOUNDATIONS OF FAITHFUL STEWARDSHIP

I n the following parable, Jesus paints a word picture of the foundations of faithful stewardship (Matthew 25:14–30):

> *Again, it will be like a man going on a journey, who called his servants and entrusted his wealth to them. To one he gave five bags of gold, to another two bags, and to another one bag, each according to his ability. Then he went on his journey. The man who had received five bags of gold went at once and put his money to work and gained five more. So also, the one with two bags of gold gained two more. But the man who had received one bag went off, dug a hole in the ground and hid his master's money.*
>
> *After a long time the master of those servants returned and settled accounts with them. The man who had received five bags of gold brought the other five. "Master," he said, "you entrusted*

me with five bags of gold. See, I have gained five more."

His master replied, "Well done, good and faithful servant! You have been faithful with a few things; I will put you in charge of many things. Come and share your master's happiness!"

The man with two bags of gold also came. "Master," he said, "you entrusted me with two bags of gold; see, I have gained two more."

His master replied, "Well done, good and faithful servant! You have been faithful with a few things; I will put you in charge of many things. Come and share your master's happiness!" Then the man who had received one bag of gold came. "Master," he said, "I knew that you are a hard man, harvesting where you have not sown and gathering where you have not scattered seed. So I was afraid and went out and hid your gold in the ground. See, here is what belongs to you."

His master replied, "You wicked, lazy servant! So you knew that I harvest where I have not sown and gather where I have not scattered seed? Well then, you should have put my money on deposit with the bankers, so that when I returned I would have received it back with interest.

"So take the bag of gold from him and give it to the one who has ten bags. For whoever has will be given more, and they will have an abundance. Whoever does not have, even what they have will be taken from him. And throw that worthless

*servant outside, into the darkness, where there
will be weeping and gnashing of teeth."*

Of course, the "man going on a journey" is Jesus, who would
soon return to heaven, and "after a long time" will return at His
Second Coming.

Notice some of Jesus' wording: "entrusting," "his wealth,"
"to his servants." This parable teaches the essence of what we
call "stewardship." In the New Testament, a person who managed the possessions of another was called a "steward."

When Jesus is our Lord, we are not our own, we belong
to Him. We became His when we individually decided to admit
"I have sinned" and "I have decided to trust in Jesus to forgive my sins and be my Savior and Lord." That was our spiritual
birth, and that birth made us His. He is our Savior and Lord.

But there is more. At the time of our salvation, God's Spirit
moved into us, never to leave. He is always present to enable
our obedience and to develop our faithful stewardship of all He
gives us. The indwelling Holy Spirit guides us and empowers us
to make good decisions: career, relationship, daily, long term,
stewardship, and the list goes on.

The Spirit of God connects us with Him and all others who
are His.

A FAITHFUL STEWARD BELIEVES GOD OWNS EVERYTHING.

God has trusted us with some of what He owns. Picture
God creating everything. He owns it all by right of being its
Creator. Over 40 times between Genesis and Revelation, the
Bible affirms that God is the Creator.

People establish ownership by recording a *deed* (a piece of paper) at the county seat or another place of public records. God's *deed*, including a legal description, is recorded in Psalm 24:1–2, "The earth is the LORD's, and everything in it, the world, and all who live in it; for he founded it on the seas and established it on the waters."

Moreover, everything rightfully belongs to God because He maintains what He created. God revealed this to Job in a very dramatic way (see Job 38–39).

FURTHERMORE, GOD IS THE OWNER OF EVERYTHING BY RIGHT OF REDEMPTION.

We rejoice that Christ redeemed us from condemnation by His own death on the Cross. The instant we trusted Him as our redeemer, we became a child of God by spiritual birth (1 Peter 1:3) and a "joint heir" with Christ of all that God has (Romans 8:17).

We take a giant step of faithful stewardship when we understand that we have received everything we have from God— like the servants in Jesus' parable. Therefore we are stewards of all we have received.

Would this be a good time to paint a mural of what God has placed in trust with you? You could start with your body, mental capabilities, talents, time, positions, possessions, relationships, prayer, every breath you draw, every heartbeat, amazing body glands and functions, employment . . . an endless list. God "gives to all *people* life and breath and all things" (Acts 17:25 NASB, also consider 1 Corinthians 4:7).

There is certainly wisdom in the word of caution God gave His chosen earthly people as they entered the Promised Land. Deuteronomy 8:11–14 says:

> Be careful that you do not forget the LORD your God, failing to observe his commands, his laws and his decrees that I am giving you this day. Otherwise, when you eat and are satisfied, when you build fine houses and settle down, and when your herds and flocks grow large and your silver and gold increase and all you have is multiplied, then your heart will become proud and you will forget the LORD your God, who brought you out of Egypt, out of the land of slavery.

A FAITHFUL STEWARD HAS MEANINGFUL PURPOSE AND FELLOWSHIP WITH GOD.

God entrusted Noah with the assignment to build an ark to save his family and life on earth. Samson and David were entrusted with strength to deliver Israel from their enemies.

The New Testament tells us: "Now there are varieties of gifts, but the same Spirit. And there are varieties of ministries, and the same Lord. There are varieties of effects, but the same God who works all things in all *persons*. But to each one is given the manifestation of the Spirit for the common good" (1 Corinthians 12:4–7 NASB).

What entrustment or opportunity has God given you? By being a faithful steward you will experience special blessings. Consider the honor: God has entrusted *you* with managing some of *His* possessions. How is that for a feeling of responsibility—and worth?

May I inject my personal testimony here? As I write this, I reflect on my own pilgrimage. Somehow I was never informed that at salvation I was a spiritual infant, designed to grow spiritually, like every newborn child of God. I thoughtlessly assumed that my salvation experience was the entire package of spiritual life.

Consequently, when I saw and heard others tell of spiritual experiences different from mine I concluded I must not have been truly saved. I struggled secretly with doubt and confusion for many years.

Eventually I became aware that spiritual infancy is part of the genuine spiritual birth experience of every saved person. I also began to notice the frank biblical record of the spiritual immaturity and subsequent spiritual growth of the apostles, especially Simon Peter, and Paul (Philippians 3:3–14).

In my uncertain condition I had wondered if I was living like a Christian. I did not know what living a "Christian life" was like. I asked several authorities and no one seemed to know the answer.

Rather late in my spiritual life I discovered that Jesus summarized the Christian life in the Great Commission (Matthew 28:19–20):

> *Therefore go and make disciples of all nations, baptizing them in the name of the Father and of the Son and of the Holy Spirit, and teaching them to obey everything I have commanded you. And surely I am with you always, to the very end of the age.*

Notice the three commands that are part of this commission: "make disciples"—the Christian life begins with becoming a disciple by spiritual birth; "baptizing them"—the first expression of the Christian life is baptism; and "teaching them to obey everything I have commanded you." I finally awoke to the fact that the third part of the Christian life comes with teaching others—and being taught ourselves—learning to obey everything Jesus commanded.

This awakening motivated me to try to learn exactly what Jesus commanded. I began looking for and listing His commands in the four Gospels. I soon discovered that His commands are not religious rules and regulations. In fact, I discovered that Jesus actually scolded people for trusting in rules, rituals, regulations, and ceremonies (see Matthew 23).

I was also enlightened by Jesus' simple yet extremely profound summary of the Old Testament commands: "'Love the Lord your God with all your heart and with all your soul and with all your mind.' This is the first and greatest commandment. And the second is like it: 'Love your neighbor as yourself.' All the Law and the Prophets hang on these two commandments" (Matthew 22:37–40).

Looking seriously at the Ten Commandments (Exodus 20:3–17), I noticed they are about relationships with God and man, not *churchy* rules and rituals. Jesus' commands are about practical issues, such as relationships in family, marriage, and among friends and enemies. He also gave liberating commands about how to handle stress, worry, and other issues of daily life.

Jesus summed up His commands: "Come to Me, all who are weary and heavy-laden, and I will give you rest. Take My yoke upon you and learn from Me, for I am gentle and humble in heart, and YOU WILL FIND REST FOR YOUR SOULS. For My yoke is easy and My burden is light" (Matthew 11:28–30 NASB).

Next, I took note of the practical commands in His Sermon on the Mount (Matthew 5:1–7:27). I found the wisdom of obeying His commands throughout life: "Everyone who comes to Me and hears My words and acts on them, I will show you whom he is like: he is like a man building a house, who dug deep and laid a foundation on the rock; and when a flood occurred, the torrent burst against that house and could not shake it, because it had been well built" (Luke 6:47–48 NASB).

After studying the Gospels, I made a list from the epistles because Jesus said to the apostles, "I have many more things to say to you, but you cannot bear *them* now. But when He, the Spirit of truth, comes, He will guide you into all the truth" (John 16:12–13 NASB).

Doing what Jesus commanded liberates us from man made churchy rituals, regulations, ceremonies. Doing what Jesus commanded is living the genuine Christian life. The bottom line: obeying Jesus' commands develops mental, social, financial, and spiritual maturity. It liberates us from oppressive rules and rituals. It produces in our lives healthy friendships, marriages, families, businesses, and a good work ethic. It develops sound minds and quality character. Moreover, it develops a thriving fellowship with God (see John 14:21, 23; 1 John 1:5–10).

FAITHFUL STEWARDSHIP IS A MAJOR KEY TO BEING PREPARED FOR JESUS' RETURN (MATTHEW 25:19-30).

Jesus told the parable of the bags of gold so that we could be prepared for His return—even if His return is "after a long time" and we have passed through death into His presence. The day for settling accounts will come (2 Corinthians 5:10). Jesus Christ, who gave His life for us and gave us everything we have, will ask us what we did with what He entrusted to us. After we have experienced the blessings of faithful stewardship on earth, we will be given royal status and reign with Christ forever (Matthew 25:34; Revelation 22:5).

WE DARE NOT IGNORE JESUS' STATEMENT ABOUT THOSE WHO REJECT STEWARDSHIP (MATTHEW 25:24-30).

This life is the training ground for eternity, and faithful stewardship is part of basic training. Why not vigorously participate?

REFLECTIONS

1. Take the time to write down how you are impacted by the fact that God entrusts you with His valuable treasures.

2. Make a list of "God's property" that has been entrusted to you.

3. When you are asked to give account to Him about how you managed His trust, what will you say?

CHAPTER 2

BE FAITHFUL WITH YOUR BODY

Therefore, I urge you, brothers and sisters, in view of God's mercy, to offer your bodies as a living sacrifice, holy and pleasing to God—this is your true and proper worship.

—ROMANS 12:1

Do you not know that your bodies are temples of the Holy Spirit, who is in you, whom you have received from God? You are not your own; you were bought at a price. Therefore honor God with your bodies.

—1 CORINTHIANS 6:19–20

For we know that if the earthly tent we live in is destroyed, we have a building from God, an eternal house in heaven, not built by human hands. . . . For while we are in this tent, we groan and are burdened, because we do not wish to be unclothed but to be clothed with our heavenly dwelling, so that what is mortal may be swallowed up by life.

—2 CORINTHIANS 5:1, 4

ave you ever wondered why God gave you a body—especially the body you have? Probably you will never know all the reasons, but one fact is obvious. Your body is essential to experiencing life in this world. Think of all the joys you would have missed if God had not given you a body. You would have missed the taste of delicious food, the beauty of a sunset, the comfort of a hug, and a thousand other pleasures. Admittedly, you would also have missed the pain that the body suffers, but even pain has benefits. God gave you the body you have for good reasons.

Since our body is so present with us and so important to us, faithful stewardship of our body must be important. Faithful stewardship requires that we accept our body as a gift from God, realize how vulnerable our body is, present our body to God as a living sacrifice, develop good bodily communication skills with the world around us, manage our body with moral integrity, and glorify God with our body. We want to be ready to give an account to God for what we did with our body when we stand before Him.

YOUR BODY IS A GIFT FROM GOD. ACCEPT IT WITH THANKSGIVING AND PRAISE!

The psalmist wrote, "For you created my inmost being; you knit me together in my mother's womb. I praise you because I am fearfully and wonderfully made; your works are wonderful, I know that full well" (Psalm 139:13–14).

Do you share the psalmist's gratitude? A good place to begin stewardship of your body is by thanking God for it. Although the body is faulty, it is an incredible creation designed to serve you well. It has a brain for thinking, feet for walking, hands for working, eyes for seeing, ears for hearing, a mouth for eating and speaking, a digestive system to secure energy and a circulatory system to deliver that energy where your body needs it, a glandular system to inject the proper chemicals at the right time, a heart for pumping blood, a liver for purifying the blood, and an immune system for fighting disease. To top it off, most of the body functions automatically!

It is fitting to recognize good qualities in a gift we receive from others. So it is proper to recognize the positive things about the body God gave you. Why spend time and energy on the imperfections of your body? Why not make a list or draw a picture of the positive features of your body and thank God for each one? You may feel a bit self-conscious, but keep in mind you are not complimenting yourself but, God, the Maker of your body. Include in your list the characteristics that distinguish you as unique from billions of other bodies in the world. Your body is an original design by God. If you are honest, your list will be quite long, a feeling of gratitude will well up in your heart, and your voice will break out in praise to your heavenly Father.

While you are working on thankfulness, also list those qualities of your body that are not so beautiful. Paul mentions them as an illustration of the church (1 Corinthians 12:22–26). All of us have beautiful parts and ugly parts. Have you ever seen a beautiful thyroid gland? Would you want your lungs on display because they are so pretty? Yet what would you do without these and other "unpresentable" parts? They are necessary and are some of your richest assets.

YOUR BODY IS A TENT. TREAT IT ACCORDINGLY!

The human body is sometimes called a tent in the Bible (2 Corinthians 5:1, 4). I heard one man call his an "earth suit." Whatever you call it, your body is a fragile dwelling place. Its usefulness can be curtailed by disease or accident, and it will eventually die. Therefore, being a faithful steward calls for taking care of your body by eating properly, exercising, and avoiding reckless risks.

I learned, the hard way (by camping) that to be comfortable in a tent you must take care of it. If you let the floor get wet, you will not sleep well. If you carry food inside, wildlife may come in. Storing your tent without drying it will cause it to mildew. If you tear it, your protection is violated. Take good care of your tent!

On the other hand, there are limits to how much money and energy should be spent on a tent. A tent is not pitched to be admired, but to be used. You can give the quest for a perfect body a higher priority than good stewardship warrants. The use of your body is the real key to good stewardship. Disease and disabilities are not our worst enemy. Sin, our worst enemy, includes both the sins of omission and commission (Matthew 10:28; Romans 1:24; 6:12).

Our primary effort, more important than diet and exercise, must be directed toward righteous use of our bodies. You will find that the best regimen for righteousness is seeking to glorify God (1 Corinthians 6:20). Joni Eareckson Tada has used her quadriplegic body to bless thousands of people through her writing, speaking, and art. On the other hand, we hear news stories of star athletes with "perfect" bodies whose lives have been destroyed because they abused their bodies with unrighteous and detrimental activities.

Faithful stewards will: take the best possible care of their "tent" for optimum usefulness; concentrate on glorifying God with their body; not lose heart when disease and pain show up; find cheer in the assurance that the afflictions of this life add to their eternal reward (2 Corinthians 4:16–18); come to terms with their "tent" and make the best of it rather than waste precious time wishing for a better one; and through faith in Christ be prepared for death at any time.

YOUR BODY IS A TEMPLE. WORSHIP WITH IT!

We live in a time when many think their bodies belong to them, and they can do whatever they please with them. It does not occur to them to acknowledge that Christ bought them with His death on the Cross. The idea of turning control of their bodies over to the Holy Spirit and glorifying God with them is not appealing. Consequently, they rush through life missing the whole point of having bodies. Physical and materialistic concerns regarding their bodies can come between them and their acceptance of Christ as Savior and Lord. The result: their "whole [bodies will] be thrown into hell" (Matthew 5:29).

Jesus commanded us to avoid giving our bodies top priority. The main concern of a faithful steward is seeking His rule and His righteousness (Luke 12:22–31). Faithful stewardship of the body begins at the point you believe in Jesus Christ as your Savior. That is your spiritual birth. Romans 12:1 NASB describes an early important stewardship decision, "Therefore I urge you, brethren, by the mercies of God, to present your bodies a living and holy sacrifice, acceptable to God, *which is* your spiritual service of worship."

When the Old Testament worshipper laid his prize animal on the altar, it never belonged to him again. The New Testament says to the faithful steward, "you are not your own" (1 Corinthians 6:19). You and your body belong to God, to be used by Him as He wills. His spirit is to occupy and control it. You can never again assert your right to do with your body as you please. Only His will is to be done with your body. Daily in every circumstance you are called to serve God as though He is incarnate in your body. In your marriage and family relationships, your body is to honor God. At work, at recreation, at church, at every moment, God is to have control. You are to take into your body only what honors God. You are to exercise and rest your body to the glory of God. All to glorify God.

The presentation of your body mentioned in Romans 12:1 is addressed to saved people, but it does not automatically happen when you are saved. It is your choice; you and you alone can make the presentation. Your parents cannot do it for you at a christening, dedication, or any other time. It could be, and probably should be, done in the privacy of your prayer closet. If, however, the Holy Spirit calls for public commitment, do it.

You present your body as a holy sacrifice that is "pleasing to God." *Holy* means set apart for God. Holiness does not eliminate the functions of work, eating, sex with your marriage partner, recreation, or any other proper bodily function. The Bible clearly presents all of those activities as "pleasing to God" when done according to His commands.

God will accept your offering as your "spiritual service of worship." He will accept it whether your body is fat or thin, tall or short, young or old, healthy or unhealthy. Worship is experiencing the presence of God, adoring Him, and bowing before Him in submission. We frequently limit worship to a church experience, but God wants us to experience Him in all of the activities of daily life. Presenting your body to God turns all of life into a worship service.

At this point, three questions are necessary:

Does the Holy Spirit dwell in your body with free and unrestricted access?

Have you presented your body to God as a living sacrifice?

And, if not, when will you?

YOUR BODY IS A VALUABLE COMMUNICATION INSTRUMENT. USE IT WISELY!

Your body enables you to relate to and communicate with people around you. Being a faithful steward includes choosing the kind and quality of your communications. You can use your tongue to praise God and tell the good news of Christ or you can blaspheme God and curse others (James 3:2–12). You can use your sexuality as a blessing to your marriage partner or for promiscuity outside marriage. You can use your hands to earn an honest living and serve humanity or to abuse others. Your eyes and ears can feed your mind with constructive information or with garbage. Wise stewardship means making good choices.

Parents, for example, find their bodies are essential to healthy communication with their children. A parent's physical presence expresses security and love. The face of each parent reflects heartfelt emotions that children recognize when they are quite young. Holding your child's hand while crossing a busy street communicates care and security. Holding a child on your lap can develop your child's sense of worth. Reading to your child will develop thinking skills, an appreciation for reading, and a readiness for successful educational pursuits. Just changing your baby's diaper promptly can lay the foundation for faith in God because it teaches your baby that someone out there responds to his cry for help. With your body you can serve a meal, write a check, make a bed, drive your little girl to school, make a dress, and do a thousand other things that express love. Your children will rise up and bless you like the children of the virtuous woman of Proverbs 31:10–31.

YOUR BODY WAS MADE TO LIVE WITHIN GODLY SEXUAL BOUNDARIES. RESPECT THEM!

We are stewards of our sexuality. Human sexuality and activity is currently a prominent and public subject: laws have been passed and courts have ruled contradictory to what the Bible teaches. So I must address this subject.

Without apology, I agree with God's position as presented in the Bible. It has been, and still is, proven true and trustworthy.

First, God has always made—and is still making—only male and female (Genesis 1:27) human beings. Moreover, He has much to say in His Word about sexual conduct: good and bad, right and wrong. His main message is that sexual activity is to be participated in by one male and one female and only within marriage (Genesis 2:22–24). Sexual activity outside the biblically defined marriage relationship is a violation labeled "adultery," "fornication," and an "abomination" (Exodus 20:14; Leviticus 18:22–23; 1 Corinthians 6:15–18) in these and many other passages throughout the Bible.

Stewardship of sexuality includes: accepting your sexual makeup, exercising disciplined control over your sexual urges and temptations, abstaining from sexual activity until marriage, being sexually true to your marriage partner (physically, psychologically, and emotionally), and meeting the sexual needs of your marriage partner (1 Corinthians 7:3–5).

Our common and prominent problem is: all of us, without exception, are sinners, violators of God's laws. As declared in many similar Bible passages:

> For all have sinned and fall short of the glory of God.
>
> —ROMANS 3:23

> The LORD has looked down from heaven upon the sons of men to see if there are any who understand, who seek after God. They have all turned aside, together they have become corrupt; there is no one who does good, not even one.
>
> — PSALM 14:2–3 NASB (SEE ALSO ROMANS 3:10.)

Not one of us is in a position to judge that we are better than anyone else. We are all guilty of one sort of sin or another.

God's perfect solution for this universal problem is forgiveness in Christ who "Himself bore our sins in His body on the cross, so that we might die to sin and live to righteousness; for by His wounds you were healed" (1 Peter 2:24 NASB). Anyone can be completely forgiven "freely by his grace through the redemption that came by Christ Jesus" (Romans 3:24). Another statement about how to be forgiven is, "If we confess our sins, He is faithful and righteous to forgive us our sins and to cleanse us from all unrighteousness" (1 John 1:9 NASB).

Our sinful nature easily causes some confusion at this point. Remember, sin means "to miss the target" of God's perfect law. In terms of sexuality, the target is male/female, the opposite sex to our physical makeup.

According to the Bible, we all inherit a sinful nature (Psalm 51:5, Romans 5:12) that affects soul, mind, spirit, and body. That sin fault line, with which we are born, causes moral confusion of one kind or another in every human being. Some are confused about their sexual nature; others have confusion over the right and wrong of lying, stealing, or another moral issue. Christ came to save us all from our sins (Matthew 1:21). Everyone, through Christ, must deal with the temptation to perversion. Accepting your sexual nature may be easier for some people than for others. The starting place is recognition of the physical construction of our body, male or female. Christ can help us develop proper acceptance from there.

God designed sexual activity for marriage. It is our means of producing children. It is also an important means of expressing intimacy between husband and wife. It is to be the most private, intimate experience of marriage. Any sexual expression—physical or emotional—outside that marital intimacy does serious damage to the marriage bond and to everyone involved. Jesus clearly taught that adultery can be committed emotionally without any physical contact (Matthew 5:27–28).

This sin of looking lustfully finds wide acceptance in our society (commercial advertising is based on it), but for a Christian it is a violation of good sexual stewardship. Faithful male stewards are responsible for how they look at women other than their wives, and faithful women stewards are responsible for dressing modestly (1 Timothy 2:9–10).

Abortion is another big issue of our day. Therefore, how can we leave the subject of sexuality without recognizing that faithful stewardship is involved in pregnancy? Today's woman is frequently told that she has a right to do with her body what she pleases. In a sense that is true; God has even granted us the right to choose sin. He has also made it clear that we are accountable for our choices, and we will live with the consequences. Faithful stewardship takes the view that we are free to do with our body only what fits the design and intent of the One who made us.

Part of a Christian's faithful stewardship of sex is the choice to remain a virgin until marriage and then to be absolutely loyal to that marriage relationship.

The laws of our country are not often used to prosecute people who engage in sexual activity outside marriage. But, the lack of prosecution does not exempt people from living with the consequences of their actions. If a pregnancy occurs, the expectant mother has consequences. An abortion alters the consequences, but does not eliminate them. She still has her conscience to deal with and the memory of the abortion and the life it ended. Many women have confessed to lifelong regrets after having an abortion. All of us are responsible to God for what we do.

The best stewardship is abstinence from sex except in marriage, a strong faith that trusts the leadership and providence of God in decisions about family size, and acceptance of any unplanned pregnancy as a gift from God (Psalm 127:3).

YOUR BODY IS A TRUST FROM GOD. GLORIFY HIM WITH IT!

The Apostle Paul asked the believers in Corinth who had tolerated some flagrant sexual sin in their church: "Do you not know that your bodies are temples of the Holy Spirit, who is in you, whom you have received from God? You are not your own; you were bought at a price. Therefore honor God with your bodies" (1 Corinthians 6:19–20).

There are infinite ways to glorify God with your body. Some athletes have used their trained body as a platform for witnessing. Esther may have been the first to use her beauty to meet the needs of others, but she was not the last. God used Samson's strong body and Lazarus's sick body to glorify Him. Lazarus became ill and died for the glory of God (John 11:4). His death provided Jesus the opportunity to raise him from the dead. That resurrection caused many to believe in Jesus Christ as their Savior! Even in sickness you can glorify God in your body. We know that God can use an aged body because He used Moses's body for 40 years after he was 80 years old (Exodus 7:7). And God will help common people like you and me to glorify Him with the body He has given us—if we are willing.

God took upon Himself a human body so He could touch and heal people, talk with them, and offer Himself on the Cross as the redeeming sacrifice for our sins (Hebrews 10:5–10).

A study of how Jesus used His body will give you an idea of how to be a good steward of your own body.

The Apostle Paul challenges us with his earnest hope that "Christ shall be magnified in my body, whether it be by life, or by death" (Philippians 1:20 KJV).

Your body is the temple of the Holy Spirit, and a temple is a place where a priest serves God. Think of it this way: you minister as a priest wherever your body is. Christian priests have two basic ministries. One is "offering spiritual sacrifices acceptable to God through Jesus Christ" (1 Peter 2:5). Spiritual sacrifices include prayers for your family, your friends, the unsaved where you work, and your neighbors. This also includes giving (Philippians 4:18) and praising God (Hebrews 13:15). The other priestly ministry is to "declare the praises of him who has called you out of darkness into his wonderful light" (1 Peter 2:9).

YOU ARE ACCOUNTABLE TO GOD FOR WHAT YOU DO WITH YOUR BODY.

For we must all appear before the judgment seat of Christ, so that each of us may receive what is due us for the things done while in the body, whether good or bad.

—2 CORINTHIANS 5:10

Jesus serves as the best example of being a faithful steward of our bodies. Consider these facts:

- Jesus accepted His physical body, though it must have felt terribly confining and limiting. Think of it: the Lord of glory, confined to the body of a helpless infant, limited to normal growth patterns, and restricted in time and space by a body. He accepted it as the gift and will of His Father (Hebrews 10:5–7).

- Jesus overcame the temptations that appealed to His bodily cravings (Matthew 4:2–4). The use of His body to do the Father's will included the Crucifixion.

- Jesus used His body to communicate with us. That was the purpose of His incarnation. Even the trials and sufferings He experienced made Him an understanding High Priest for all believers (Hebrews 4:14–16).

- Jesus fulfilled life in His body, submitted to death in His body, and trusted God to raise it from the dead.

- Jesus glorified His Father with His body in His life, death, and Resurrection. He was never selfish with it. He used it freely, as the Father directed, to minister to the needs of people.

Despite how well you care for your body, even if you are an excellent steward of your body, it is subject to disease and malfunction. It is destined for death and the grave (Hebrews 9:27). But we who are saved will receive a new body at the Resurrection (1 Corinthians 15:50–57). It will be like Christ's body (Philippians 3:21; 1 John 3:1–3).

Never allow your body to become your master. Keep your body in its place, sexually and every other way. The Apostle Paul wrote that just as athletes discipline their bodies for winning a competition, Christians must discipline their bodies for winning the spiritual prize (1 Corinthians 9:24–27). If you indulge the desires of your flesh, those desires will take charge of you and make you their slave (Ephesians 2:3).

In the parable of the bags of gold (Matthew 25:14–30), the one who received five bags of gold managed them well and gained five more. He was commended for that stewardship (vv. 16, 20–21). Proper stewardship of your body will bear compound interest, and you will receive additional blessings and rewards.

REFLECTIONS

1. Have you completely accepted the body that God gave you? If not, why not? Take the time to accept it now.

2. Write your own personal plan for being a good steward of your body, your "tent."

3. If you have not already done so, take the time now to present your body to God as a living sacrifice and as a temple to be occupied by His Spirit.

4. List ways your body glorifies God. Ask God to open your understanding to ways you had not thought of before.

CHAPTER 3

BE FAITHFUL WITH YOUR MIND

Those who live according to the flesh have their minds set on what that nature desires; but those who live in accordance with the Spirit have their minds set on what the Spirit desires. The mind governed by the flesh is death, but the mind governed by the Spirit is life and peace. The mind governed by the flesh is hostile to God; it does not submit to God's law, nor can it do so.

—ROMANS 8:5–7

Do not conform to the pattern of this world, but be transformed by the renewing of your mind. Then you will be able to test and approve what God's will is—his good, pleasing and perfect will.

—ROMANS 12:2

Therefore, with minds that are alert and fully sober, set your hope on the grace to be brought to you when Jesus Christ is revealed at his coming.

—1 PETER 1:13 NKJV

*Let this mind be in you which was also in Christ
Jesus, who, being in the form of God, did not consider it robbery to be equal with God, but made
himself of no reputation, taking the form of a
bondservant, and coming in the likeness of men.
And being found in appearance as a man, He hum-
bled Himself and became obedient to the point
of death, even the death of the cross. Therefore
God also has highly exalted Him and given Him the
name which is above every name.*

—PHILIPPIANS 2:5–9 KJV

The word *mind* occurs many times in the Bible, in both the Old Testament and New Testament.

The mind has great spiritual significance. For example, the greatest commandment of all, according to Jesus, involves the mind. He said, "Love the Lord your God with all your heart and with all your soul and with all your mind" (Matthew 22:37). Added importance springs from the fact that "the renewing of your mind" is how you are transformed from conformity with the world to conformity with the Spirit (Romans 12:2).

Because the primary battleground with Satan is our mind, it is puzzling that today's brand of Christianity expresses little interest in the mind. The focus is on feeling good. We assign our heart to God and our mind to circumstance and chance. We seem to believe that we were handed this lame mind and can do nothing about it. Why do we take such a fatalistic view of our mental condition?

The mind, according to the Bible, is a rich, pliable gift. Several Hebrew and Greek words are translated *mind*. Biblical definitions of the mind include: faculties of perceiving, understanding, thinking, feeling, deciding, desiring, meditating, imagining, and remembering. How about hope, depression, perception, and opinions? And don't overlook purpose, passion, compassion, and determination. Did I leave out *love*? To that list the Bible adds concepts such as the inner man, the will, and the heart. Then the Bible expands the term into mindsets such as like-minded, sober-minded, sound-minded, ready-minded, double-minded, and humble-minded.

Each of us is a steward/manager of our own mind.

WE ARE BORN WITH A NATURAL MIND.

We begin our life with this natural mind (Romans 8:6–7) and early in life begin to develop our own unique version of this natural mind. Through the years we develop a complex mental program to handle all of the information received and stored. We use that program to reason, solve problems, make plans, worry, imagine, make decisions, develop attitudes, act, and react. We use that program to decide what appetites to satisfy (Ephesians 2:3), what emotions to feel, and to determine our priorities and values. Every experience of life is stored in our natural mind. Some information was deposited without our consent. Other information is there because we chose to watch, listen, read, or experience something.

The good steward carefully screens what the mind is exposed to. Frequently people discussing a current movie say, "It's a good movie, except for a few scenes." Take note: the not-so-good scenes were stored with the good scenes in the memories of those who watched it.

The natural mind is easily and seriously flawed by sin and desires that are sinful. A study of Romans 8:5–8 gives us valuable insight into the problems of the natural mind. The natural mind is set on the things of the flesh, the New Testament word for our un-regenerated nature, which we have from birth.

The flesh is interested in physical needs such as food, drink, sex, and shelter; safety and security needs such as locked doors and savings in the bank; social needs such as love and acceptance; and self-esteem needs such as recognition, fame, and/or fulfillment.

All of these needs have been perverted and corrupted by sin. Therefore, the works of the flesh fall into the following categories: "sexual immorality, impurity and debauchery; idolatry and witchcraft; hatred, discord, jealousy, fits of rage, selfish ambition, dissensions, factions and envy; drunkenness, orgies, and the like" (Galatians 5:19–21). This is why Romans 8:6 says bluntly that "the mind governed by the flesh is death."

"The mind set on the flesh is hostile toward God" (Romans 8:7 NASB). This explains why men with natural, fleshly minds crucified Christ and why Saul of Tarsus persecuted Christians before he met Christ on the Damascus Road. It also explains why one afternoon as I told a man about how much God loved him, he rose up in a rage as if he wanted to attack me. His fleshly mind was hostile toward God.

"The mind set on the flesh . . . does not subject itself to the law of God" (v. 7 NASB). A mind set on the flesh may give lip service to the law and commands of God, but it will not obey them. In fact, the flesh *cannot* obey God's law. The mind set on the flesh is the mind of the unsaved, un-regenerated person who has never received Jesus Christ as personal Savior. Therefore, "those who are in the flesh cannot please God" (v. 8 NASB). It is not that God is too hard to please. The word cannot means "no power." The flesh has no power to do what pleases God, even if it wanted to please Him.

The natural mind is not capable of understanding the things of the Spirit of God (1 Corinthians 2:14) and is blinded to the gospel of Christ (2 Corinthians 4:3–4). That mind does not have faith in God and is prone to worry and anxiety (Matthew 6:31–32). Its imaginations are "futile" (Romans 1:21). A futile imagination caused the rich fool to think his wealth would satisfy the needs of his soul (Luke 12:16–19).

Moreover, the natural mind uses flawed and inferior problem-solving skills. It often blames others for problems. Many people waste a lifetime blaming their parents or some other person for their problems. Yes, parents can cause children to have low self-esteem, but blaming them does not raise self-esteem. Progress is possible only if we take responsibility for the choices we make. Taking responsibility must be followed quickly with a decision to move forward under the Lordship of Christ in the power He supplies.

EVERY PERSON WHO RECEIVES JESUS AS SAVIOR AND LORD IS GIVEN A SPIRITUAL MIND.

The spiritual mind is a new mind that becomes ours through the regeneration that God works in us when we turn from sin and trust Christ as our personal Savior. Its "newness" speaks primarily to its quality and difference from the natural mind. Newness in time is incidental.

The new spiritual mind is set on "the things of the Spirit" (Romans 8:5 NASB). A new capacity for spiritual understanding becomes ours at spiritual birth when the Holy Spirit begins to indwell us (John 14:17). He resides in us to teach us all things and guide us into all truth (John 14:25–26; 16:13). The Holy Spirit motivates us to seek spiritual and eternal values.

Through renewing of the mind, saved people are transformed from conformity to this world (Romans 12:2). I fear that many Christians have overlooked this. They do not know this transforming secret. They try to shed their conformity to this world through their own willpower and effort while still operating out of the old fleshly mindset. Isn't it strange that we seem to think salvation only applies to our heart and soul? We assume that our mind needs to change very little, when in fact every aspect of it needs to change.

Failure to pursue the renewing of our mind causes us to slip back into old feelings and old ways of thinking. Our old mind was not erased; the old tapes still play. Unhealthy mental conditions spawned in our unsaved life demand control. We learn from the Apostle Peter that a saved person can operate out of the fleshly mind. At one point he fell back into thinking the old way. Jesus rebuked Peter because he was not mindful of the things of God but only the things of men (Matthew 16:23). Even after the great day of Pentecost he reverted to fleshly thinking (Galatians 2:11–14).

To allow the natural mind to dominate us after we are saved will cause spiritual shipwreck. If we make no effort to nurture and develop the spiritual mind, the natural mind will continue to feed itself on what is available. There is plenty of mental junk food around. Commercials and entertainment on TV appeal to the natural mind. It is natural for us to desire the products that promise happiness, satisfaction, youth, and beauty. It is also natural for us to develop guilt and low self-esteem because we cannot purchase all of those products. We are often tempted as we see sin portrayed as enjoyable. The dominant mindset of our society is the natural mind. Even some religions appeal to the natural mind by presenting rules and rituals as the savior. Many new "Christian" movements appeal to the natural mind. They tell us we can successfully become spiritual using our natural mind. Some suggest that we can change reality with our natural mind. But the natural mind travels a dead-end street and will eventually self-destruct.

GOOD NEWS: YOUR MIND CAN BE RENEWED!

I gained a new understanding of this truth when a psychiatrist visited me in my office. Joy radiated from her face as she told me about her new faith in Christ. Her testimony was clear and biblical as she expressed her desire to obey her Lord in baptism, church membership, and daily service. With excitement, this fully-trained, practicing psychiatrist said, "I enjoy Bible study so much because the Bible contains so much mental health."

Every saved person has the capacity to be transformed through the renewing of the mind. Salvation begins with a change of mind (repentance). The Spirit of God awakens our heart to our sinfulness. Our heart calls upon our mind to change. Before that turning, in our unbelief, we are full of bad attitudes, desires, priorities, values, imaginations, and affections. When we turn from unbelief to faith, God regenerates us, gives us a new heart, and begins the process of renewing our mind.

Our mind can be reprogrammed. Paul went into the Arabian Desert soon after his conversion (Galatians 1:17) to get a jump start on this renewal. His ideas of God, Christ, grace, faith, true righteousness, and many other issues were completely changed.

New spiritual thinking can replace old "fleshly" thinking. Can you recall some of the bad stories we listened to and even repeated before we became serious about making Jesus Lord? I can. Those memories seem to surface at such embarrassing times. I wish I could erase them, but we do not have the power of selective forgetfulness.

Someone told me that it is easier to remember than forget. I challenged his statement. He replied, "Think of a number." I put 436 into my mind. He asked me to repeat the number. I said, "436."

Then he said, "Now forget it." Of course, I could not choose to forget the number. We cannot exercise selective forgetting, but we can exercise selective recall and choose the material for our meditation.

When unwanted thoughts arise we can send them back to their dungeon and replace them with healthy thoughts. The Bible gives us this excellent formula: "Finally, brothers and sisters, whatever is true, whatever is noble, whatever is right, whatever is pure, whatever is lovely, whatever is admirable—if anything is excellent or praiseworthy—think about such things" (Philippians 4:8). This eight-layered screen filters out depressive, destructive, deceptive, demeaning, unjust, impure, love-destroying, embarrassing, inferior, and blaming thoughts. Please note: development of the renewed mind is a lifelong process. Jesus promised believers that "the Holy Spirit, whom the Father will send in my name, will teach you all things and will remind you of everything I have said to you" (John 14:26). As life unfolds, the Holy Spirit will help the saved person develop the thought patterns, or mindset program, of the renewed mind.

We can develop a healthy mindset only with Christ. The good news from God can replace the bad news stored up in the old mind. Mary, the mother of Jesus, is a good example. After the shepherds reported to her the things the angel and the heavenly host told them about Jesus, she "pondered them in her heart" (Luke 2:19). *Thayer's Greek–English Lexicon* tells us that *pondered* in this context means "to bring together in one's mind, confer with oneself." She brought the good news from the shepherds and her other thoughts together and let it rearrange her former thinking.

The Bible also affirms that the saved person can have a sound mind. When Jesus finished with the man of Gadara, the citizens of the country observed him "sitting there, dressed and in his right mind" (Mark 5:15). We are also assured that "God has not given us a spirit of fear, but of power and of love and of a sound mind" (2 Timothy 1:7 NKJV). A sound mind includes self-control. With His help we can gain control of our thoughts.

In Christ, we can have a growing mind. We begin with very little knowledge. Information is added to information, decisions are added to decisions, feelings are added to feelings, and a network develops. That is true of our natural mind, and it is true of our spiritual mind. It is a sad thing to find a spiritually stunted Christian. Lack of spiritual growth is the product of poor stewardship.

Believe it! You can be transformed through the renewing of your mind. You are not locked into the old thought patterns, no matter how long they have been there or how deeply they are ingrained.

GOD ASSIGNS US RESPONSIBILITY FOR OUR MINDS.

"Love the Lord your God with all your heart and with all your soul and with all your mind." This is the first and greatest commandment.

MATTHEW 22:37–38

The relative measure of your IQ is not the issue here. All of the mind you have and what you do with it is the issue. Entertain only thoughts that are compatible with love for God. Don't forget that God's love is both tender and tough.

Feed your mind on every suggestion of God's love for you, His faithfulness to you, His wise and compassionate dealings with you. Read about it in the Bible, make it the meditation into which your idle mind naturally slips, sing about it quietly in your heart. Spend time in meditation, prayer, and thanksgiving at the Cross where God forever settled that He loves you. Daily thank the Father and thank Christ for His great love for you.

Reject every idea, suggestion, or thought that slanders or doubts God. Satan is a slanderer; his main work is to slander God. He slandered God to Eve in the Garden of Eden, and he cunningly slanders God today. He will present to you a circumstance and then suggest that God has failed, thus tempting you to turn against God. Satan tried it with Job and will try it with you.

Make every mental function obedient to Christ. Our instruction is to demolish arguments and every pretension that sets itself up against the knowledge of God. We are to take captive every thought to make it obedient to Christ (2 Corinthians 10:5). Demolish all thought patterns, systems of logic, and problem solving techniques that are contrary to the teaching of Christ. Ask Christ to help you develop His way of reasoning and solving problems.

Take captive the unresolved problems of the past that enslave you by dealing with them as Jesus instructed. Seek reconciliation with others through confrontation, confession, apology, and love. Peter is a good example of this. On the night Jesus was betrayed, as Peter was thinking with the old mind, he denied he even knew Christ. Fortunately, God used Peter's memory to motivate him to deal with that sin. After the cock crowed, Peter remembered that Jesus had warned him this would happen. Peter broke down and wept (see Mark 14:66–72). He could easily have concluded he was a hopeless failure and remained in a guilt-ridden condition for the rest of his life. He could have blamed others, circumstances—even Jesus. He chose to admit his wrong, took responsibility for his actions, and turned back to Christ. In dealing with his past, Peter found forgiveness and hope for a great future. With the help of Christ, take your emotions captive. Ask Him to give you the control He used on His own emotions.

Our stewardship of mind calls for us to study and learn. New spiritual information has to be loaded in. Jesus said: "Take my yoke upon you and learn from me" (Matthew 11:29). Jesus' favorite name for his followers was *disciple*, which includes the idea of being a student. So, we must learn new thought patterns and problem-solving skills.

We need to learn God's ways in every area of our life. Parents need to study and learn about how to be good parents. Husbands and wives need to study and learn how to develop a good marriage. Every Christian needs to study and learn how to be a better witness. All teachers and leaders in the church need to study and learn how to do their work more effectively. We all need to learn how to successfully handle the changes and surprises of life.

Jesus instructed us to not be anxious or worry over the needs of life. He assured us that our Father in heaven will take care of all our needs if we give attention to seeking His kingdom and His will (Matthew 6:25–33). Jesus conducted His life by faith in God's Word and the power of the Holy Spirit. Recall how He slept calmly in the boat on the stormy sea. You can experience that same tranquility. "Do not be anxious about anything, but in every situation, by prayer and petition, with thanksgiving, present your requests to God. And the peace of God, which transcends all understanding, will guard your hearts and your minds in Christ Jesus" (Philippians 4:6–7).

While I was looking at the Sermon on the Mount, I noted that some people make the tragic mistake of trying to use Jesus' commands as if they were magic words, that when repeated could produce special blessings. For example, this is how some churches and denominations view and recite the Lord's Prayer (Matthew 6:9–15). The truth is that Jesus, the ultimate authority on prayer, gave us the Lord's Prayer passage to instruct us on what to pray for and how to pray.

Notice Jesus' preceding statement: "And when you are praying, do not use meaningless repetition as the Gentiles do, for they suppose that they will be heard for their many words.

So do not be like them; for your Father knows what you need before you ask Him" (vv. 7–8 NASB).

It is noteworthy that there is no record that Jesus ever recited this as a prayer. He was giving His disciples (and us) an excellent outline for praying, not one to recite verbatim.

According to Jesus, the first purpose of prayer is to recognize who God is and connect with Him. He is the perfect "Father" who is in heaven and available to us. He knows what we need before we pray and is ready and able to answer our prayer and meet our needs (any and all) (Matthew 6:8). When we pray, we open the door for God to become involved in our life and circumstances.

The first petition of the Lord's Prayer is that God will take charge, that His will be done with our requests, "on earth as it is in heaven."

The second petition is for our daily material and financial needs, simply asking God to "give us this day our daily bread." This presupposes we will have a close daily fellowship with our Father in heaven.

Next, we have the wonderful opportunity to be forgiven all the sins we have committed "as we have forgiven" others. This is a reminder that being forgiven and forgiving others are closely connected. Offenses need to be dealt with quickly and consistently. God commands us to forgive and is ready to help us forgive. Since Jesus never sinned, this is further evidence that this is not a prayer Jesus prayed for Himself.

Verse 14 reminds us that we are weak in our own strength and need God's help in resisting temptation.

This model prayer includes some of Jesus' teaching about the way we communicate our needs and requests to God; and, as a result, how we practice peace and trust, focusing our hearts and minds on the sustaining grace of God.

Meditation, a strong, healthy mental process, was not invented by Eastern religions. It is as old as the book of Genesis (Genesis 24:63). We all meditate. Some call it worry, some call it daydreaming, some call it deep thought or other names. Meditation on the wrong material can lead to destruction. On the other hand, the Bible promises great peace and prosperity to those who meditate on God's Word (Psalm 1:1–3).

"Therefore gird up the loins of your mind" (1 Peter 1:13 NKJV) is an interesting command. New Testament people understood the metaphor. They wore long flowing garments tied around the waist with a girdle (belt). When an emergency came, they would quickly gather up those flowing robes, tying them together with the girdle so they would not be hindered from running or taking other swift action.

Our minds tend to be like those freely flowing robes, twisting around us, hindering us from victoriously handling life. Past abuse trips up our self-worth. Fears lock us in a terrifying prison. Unreconciled relationships cripple joy with bitterness and guilt. Selfish insecurity expressed as jealousy sabotages marriage. Depressive thoughts shackle the mind in a dark room of despair. Doubts like these keep us from experiencing peace of mind:

- "Am I really saved?"
- "Is my husband faithful?"
- "Is my job secure?"
- "Did God really create us?"
- "Is the Bible trustworthy?"
- "Does God truly exist?"

Good stewardship calls for us to get together all of our loose, harmful thought patterns and put them under the control of Christ. Take heart; there is solid hope. You can gird up your mind. The Bible affirms that our minds can be renewed. Girding up your mind is an essential part of that renewing. This *mind girdle* is woven from seven strong fibers identified in 1 Peter 1 and 2:

1. **Be self-controlled and sober (1:13).** We cannot be good stewards of our minds if we intoxicate them with alcohol or drugs.

2. **Set your hope on God's grace (1:13).** God has given us hope founded on the Resurrection of Christ and focused on the grace Christ will bring us when He returns. We have never been, nor are we yet, worthy of living forever with the holy God in the perfect heaven. Here is our hope: when Christ comes, He will bring us all the grace we need to fit us for that glory.

3. **Desire to be holy (1:14–15).** Just as a child wants to be like a parent, we are to desire to be like God. We are to stop obeying the former lusts of our old sinful nature and, at every temptation, decide to be an obedient child of our Father in heaven. As God is holy, upright in character, maintaining unimpeachable integrity, morally pure in thought and action, we are to be holy in all our behavior.

4. **Fear God (1:17).** Do these words trouble you? Some fears are proper. The person who works with high-voltage electricity must have a healthy fear of coming in contact with a live wire.

Stop and think about it: we conduct much of our lives out of fear. For example, we fear financial ruin so we work; we fear embarrassment so we dress up. However, our fears are off target due to our sinfulness. Though many of our fears are unfounded and damaging, when we fear God, unwarranted fears fade away and legitimate fears arrange themselves properly. When we fear God, we find we have nothing to fear! We have nothing to fear from Him who loves us enough to die for us. He will never abuse us. We discover we have nothing to fear from any other source; He is our shield and deliverer.

5. **Remember Christ redeemed you with His blood (1:18–19).** By paying the supreme price, Jesus declared us extremely valuable to God. We are more obligated to Him than anyone or anything else.

6. **Love the brethren fervently (1:22).** The love named here is completely unselfish in its practical care for others. It is the word used in John 3:16 to name God's love for us, love that moved Him to give His only begotten Son to save us. Great refreshment comes to the person who loves like this.

7. **Desire the sincere milk of God's Word (2:2).** Our desire for God's Word should be like a newborn baby's all-consuming desire for milk. The baby does not care what or whom he interrupts to satisfy that desire. And a baby has no desire for money, power, or fame. We should have this same kind of desire to feed our minds, hearts, and souls on the Bible so that we may grow strong toward maturity.

Permit God to develop an unselfish mind in you. We read "let this mind be in you, which was also in Christ Jesus" (Philippians 2:5 KJV). The word for mind here involves attitude. Jesus gave up His status of equality with God in order to be our Savior. He gave up His position as King of Glory and took the lowest of all positions, that of a servant. Jesus gave up His control of everything and became obedient, even obeying those who plotted and carried out His Crucifixion. "He was oppressed and afflicted, yet he did not open his mouth; he was led like a lamb to the slaughter, and as a sheep before its shearers is silent, so he did not open his mouth" (Isaiah 53:7). He did all of this to serve and save us. Therefore, God has highly exalted Him and His name above all others. The path to the renewed mind leads through service. Dark days may come while serving, but the end of the journey is glory.

Stewardship of the mind begins with salvation. It continues as the saved person pursues the renewing of the mind. That pursuit will call for listening, self-denial, reading, seeking Christian counsel, and making tough choices and changes. But the outcome will be transformation!

REFLECTIONS

1. Review this chapter, underlining characteristics of the natural mind.

2. Identify areas of your mind that need to be renewed.

3. List actions you can take to renew your mind.

4. List the seven fibers of the "mind girdle" for the renewed mind.

CHAPTER 4

BE FAITHFUL WITH YOUR ABILITIES

There are different kinds of gifts, but the same Spirit distributes them. There are different kinds of service, but the same Lord. There are different kinds of working, but in all of them and in everyone it is the same God at work. Now to each one the manifestation of the Spirit is given for the common good. To one there is given through the Spirit a message of wisdom, to another a message of knowledge by means of the same Spirit, to another faith by the same Spirit, to another gifts of healing by that one Spirit, to another miraculous powers, to another prophecy, to another distinguishing between spirits, to another speaking in different kinds of tongues, and to still another the interpretation of tongues. All these are the work of one and the same Spirit, and he distributes them to each one, just as he determines.

—1 CORINTHIANS 12:4–11

Do you have a God-given ability that could both help people and glorify Jesus Christ? Before you say no, let me ask you some other questions. Can you walk or talk? Do you have ears and eyes, hands and feet? Is your head bald or covered with hair? You will probably say, "Of course, but those are characteristics we all have in common." Is it possible you are overlooking a vital area of stewardship just because it is "common"?

ALL ABILITIES ARE GIFTS OF GOD.

It is written that God "gives everyone life and breath and everything else" (Acts 17:25). So the ability to breathe, walk, talk, think, speak, and all other common abilities are gifts of God. Receiving a gift from God makes us a steward of that gift.

We can learn from the lad David, son of Jesse. When he volunteered to fight Goliath, King Saul said, "You are not able to go out against this Philistine and fight him; you are only a young man, and he has been a warrior from his youth" (1 Samuel 17:33). Notice the word *able*. David responded by telling Saul how he had killed a lion and a bear that attacked the sheep. Then David added: "The LORD who rescued me from the paw of the lion and the paw of the bear will rescue me from the hand of this Philistine" (v. 37). David gave God the credit for his ability to defeat the lion and the bear, and he counted on His help to defeat Goliath.

Later he wrote: "Praise be to the LORD my Rock, who trains my hands for war, my fingers for battle" (Psalm 144:1). You may think that it would be difficult to honor God with an ability to fight. That is exactly the point. All abilities come from God and can be used to glorify Him. The Bible affirms that King David used His God-given fighting ability to fulfill the purposes of God in liberating the oppressed Israelites.

A few years ago I learned a new appreciation for the gift of walking. One morning, a few minutes after breakfast, the room began to spin. For several weeks, I had experienced some attacks of dizziness that lasted only a few seconds. I thought this was just another attack and would soon pass.

I was standing by the kitchen sink, so I leaned against the cabinet and slid to a sitting position on the floor, but the attack did not go away. Even with my eyes closed, I felt like I was spinning around. I crawled a few feet to the carpeted floor of the next room and fell flat on the floor.

Three hours later I was still lying on the floor with my head spinning, so I asked my son to dial 911. The hospital did some tests and diagnosed the problem as an acute case of labyrinthitis, an illness in which the inner ear becomes inflamed, causing nausea and a loss of balance. It was apparently due to a virus.

My son took me back to his house with my head still spinning. About midnight I awoke and realized the spinning had stopped. Thinking I was OK, I crawled out of bed and tried to stand up. I fell flat on the floor. My sense of balance was gone. For two weeks the best I could do was crawl on the floor. The first time I was able to struggle to a standing position, I thanked God.

I learned that just being able to stand up and walk is a precious gift. Jesus' statement "apart from me you can do nothing" (John 15:5) took on new meaning for me. Every ability is an important gift!

EVERYONE HAS COMMON ABILITIES.

The mix of abilities is different with each of us. Even if some common abilities, such as walking, seeing, or hearing are missing, you and I have a host of other abilities. These common abilities equip us for the routines of daily life.

When these common abilities are placed in the hands of Christ, daily routines become acts of ministry and service. Cleaning house can become something you do with love for your family, guests, and Christ. Using your ears to listen carefully to others can honor Christ and bless lives.

Remember the little girl, a captive from Israel, who served the wife of Naaman, commander of the army of Aram? When Naaman was afflicted with leprosy, the girl told his wife about the prophet in Israel who could heal him. A common girl spoke simple words, a prominent man listened to her, and his life was changed (read the story in 2 Kings 5:1–14)!

Any ability, no matter how small, can be used to glorify God and inspire others. It was true in Bible times. A little boy had only a lunch of five loaves and two fish, but in the hands of Jesus his lunch fed more than 5,000 people and became one of the most talked-about miracles of all time (John 6:1–14).

What was true in Bible times is also true today. Lauren attended college with me. She was a radiant Christian even though she was confined to a wheelchair. Traveling from class to class and floor to floor was difficult for her. But every time I saw Lauren, she had a radiant smile. None of us ever heard her complain. She had the ability to smile during very trying times. We were all inspired by her. Across the years, when I have severe difficulties, I remember Lauren's smile and am inspired to carry on. An everyday smile may be much more powerful than you think.

There was a woman in my hometown during my teen years who was a good cook. She made plain food, nothing fancy. She also had a heart to serve Christ by ministering to others. When she heard of someone who needed an emotional lift, she would bake a cake or cookies and quietly leave it for them to find. She would leave a note, "Given in the name of our Blessed Lord." Her cooking never won a prize at the county fair, but it did win many people to Christ because she loved enough to do what she could. She showed us that the New Testament Christianity of Dorcas is still alive. Dorcas glorified Christ and won others to Him with her needle and thread (Acts 9:36–42). Dorcas did not sit around and long for some notable talent with which to serve her Lord; she simply made garments for the widows in her town, Joppa. Faithfulness in using her needle to show love made a difference in Joppa.

When Dorcas suddenly died, the Apostle Peter was called in to help. He found the widows grieving and talking about her loving deeds. Through God's power, Peter raised Dorcas to life. The Bible records the results with these words: "This became known all over Joppa, and many people believed in the Lord" (Acts 9:42). Yes, we are stewards of even the common abilities God has trusted to us.

SOME PEOPLE HAVE UNCOMMON ABILITIES.

I knew a man who could take a knife and carve an ordinary piece of wood into a work of art. He was not handsome. His clothes sagged in disarray on his shapeless body. There was no evidence that his IQ was above average, and he was not charismatic. But he had an unusual talent for carving wood.

When God instructed Moses how to build the tabernacle, He said, "See I have chosen Bezalel . . . and I have filled him with the Spirit of God, with wisdom, with understanding, with knowledge and with all kinds of skills—to make artistic designs for work in gold, silver, and bronze, to cut and set stones, to work in wood, and to engage in all kinds of crafts. Moreover, I have appointed Oholiab . . . to help him. Also I have given ability to all the skilled workers to make everything I have commanded you" (Exodus 31:2–6). God gave those men uncommon abilities to work with metal, jewels, and other construction materials.

Does it seem strange that being filled with the Spirit of God can be connected with cutting stones and carving wood? God's Spirit can turn a talent into a ministry!

Some people today have uncommon abilities. Some perform surgery, others skillfully practice law, and still others excel in sports, music, or making money. None of these are considered holy activities, but—under the control of God's Spirit—they become holy. The battle for the souls of men, women, youth, and children is raging in the everyday world. It rages in the entertainment world, the business world, the legal world, the medical world, and every area of daily life. Christ needs soldiers on those battlefields, using their God-given uncommon abilities to minister and witness to the truth of God. That's faithful stewardship!

HIDING OR DENYING AN ABILITY IS BEING UNFAITHFUL.

In the parable at the beginning of this book, the man who received one bag of gold buried it in the ground (Matthew

25:24–25). He probably thought it was too small to matter. His grave mistake surfaced when the master came to settle accounts with his servants. His unused bag of gold was taken from him, and he was cast out. Whatever that means, it was not good. Only those who honestly admitted they had received a gift and used it were rewarded.

EVERY SAVED PERSON HAS AT LEAST ONE BODY GIFT.

A "body gift" is a gift given to you by God for the building up of the body of Christ. These spiritual gifts equip a Christian to render special service as a member of a church. Every saved person has a special ability for serving in a church (1 Corinthians 12:7). If you have been saved, you have a body gift. You may not know what it is, you may have never heard of it before, but you have at least one gift.

There are many different kinds of gifts. You will find several lists in Scripture (Romans 12:6–8; 1 Corinthians 12:8–10, 28; Ephesians 4:11). Every church has different needs, and every church needs different gifts. All churches need people who smile, are friendly, care for children, write, grow flowers, hoe weeds, run sound systems, clean floors, give money, paint walls, teach, sing, play music, and preach. You will find your gift(s) when you are ready to obey what the Holy Spirit wants you to do with it (them).

Dixie had a nice car. The church had several elderly widow members who were unable to drive. Dixie used her car like a taxi to take those widows to the mall or grocery store. They were helped, the church prospered, and Dixie was happy.

Madeline is a retired secretary who loves to write letters. She writes letters to missionaries, former church members, and anyone else who has an interest in the church. Madeline also mails a card to every church member on their birthday. She pays for this ministry herself. She is a blessing to many people.

God has gifted you to fulfill His unique purposes for you, others, and for His church. The Holy Spirit bestows the gifts. They do not come from any human source. The Holy Spirit gives these gifts and empowers us to use them. The gifts differ, but the one and same Spirit gives them (1 Corinthians 12:1–11). He is sovereign in bestowing body gifts.

"The body is not made up of one part but of many" (v. 14). Just as the human body has many members, the church has many members. No two members have the same responsibility. They may have similar responsibilities such as teaching, ushering, or singing, but each has a special application of that responsibility. For example, we can see and read with just one eye, but the other eye enhances vision and adds depth perception. If one member of the physical body decides to stop functioning because it thinks its job is not very important, the body is handicapped. Many churches limp along with handicaps because some members are not exercising their gifts (see vv. 12–31).

The gifts are given "for the common good" (v. 7). Your gift is not given for your selfish enjoyment or use, but to equip you for a unique service in your church. You are to use it for the good of the entire church. For example, when my body says it is hungry, my mind tells my feet to take me to the dinner table, my hands use the fork to put the food in my mouth, my mouth chews the food and sends it to my stomach where digestion begins, and my entire body is strengthened. None of the many members of my body exists for themselves alone. So it is in the church body.

The Bible presents the church as the context for using our gifts and talents. Your hands, feet, eyes, and heart work in the context of your body. The body parts must be closely knit together to function. A hand cannot serve the body if it is detached from the body. The parts must work together in harmony to accomplish anything. Also, if the body parts compete and are not coordinated, the body is dysfunctional. When the members of the church apply their gifts in harmony, the body is built up (Ephesians 4:16).

YOU WILL BE BLESSED BY DISCOVERING AND USING YOUR GIFT(S).

In John 4 Jesus waited at Jacob's well in a town named Sychar and talked with a woman there while the disciples went to buy food. When they returned they said to Jesus, "Rabbi, eat something." Jesus replied, "I have food to eat that you know nothing about." They wondered where He got this secret food. "My food," said Jesus, "is to do the will of him who sent me and to finish his work" (vv. 31–34).

Jesus had been walking for hours, and it was past mealtime. The woman who came to draw water had just been saved after He talked with her. Jesus was so intent on doing the will of God that He lost His physical hunger. His needs were met as He served His Father. That is true for us. When we use our abilities to serve Christ, our needs are met! You could call this one of the perks of faithful stewardship.

You are responsible for only the gifts you have, but you are responsible for all the gifts you have. In the parable of the bags of gold, each person received a different number of bags. But each was responsible for only what he was given.

Discovering your gift is very important. The Holy Spirit assigns you responsibility when He bestows the gift. Your blessings begin when you discover the gift and begin to exercise it. Both you and God's Spirit have a role in discovering your gifts. Your role includes a thankful attitude and a willingness to use your gifts for God's purpose and glory. The Spirit's role is to reveal to you what you need to know when you need to know it. Be patient; Moses was 80 years old when God revealed His assignment for delivering Israel. A word of caution: carefully avoid envying the gifts of another or looking with disdain on the gifts God has given you.

As we strive to understand how God has gifted us, we are blessed to have access to a dynamic relationship and fellowship with Him. Prayer is a good place to start. First, admit to yourself and then to God that He has given you at least one ability or gift. Tell Him you believe His Word, and since you know He is no respecter of persons, you believe He gave gifts to you. Thank Him, by faith, for being so gracious to you and for all the gifts you have received, although you may not yet know what they are.

Two common ways to discover your abilities are to find an activity that appeals to your interests and listen to what your fellow Christians say about your gifts. They may see an ability in you before you do. Also, check out the activities that you enjoy; if this is a gift from God, He will bless your efforts. Discovery of God's gifts can be very rewarding, somewhat like opening gifts at Christmas. All gifts of God are wonderful, even those that do not seem wonderful on the surface. For example, I knew a preacher in Texas who had an unusually large head, and it was bald. He told me that at first he was ashamed of his head, but then he realized it distinguished him from others. So he turned this "gift" into a tool for witnessing. He developed a good sense of humor and frequently made jokes about his bald head. God used that humor to help people feel comfortable in his otherwise intimidating presence. His sense of humor opened witnessing opportunities.

It is also very important to seek training that will sharpen the use of your gift or ability. Keep in mind that Jesus chose the 12 and gifted them to be apostles. Then He spent three years training them with such intense activity that at times they had no time to eat their meals. A dull axe is still an axe, but a sharp axe will cut more wood with less effort than a dull axe.

When you discover your gifts and exercise them, three wonderful things begin to happen: the church will be blessed, Christ will be honored, and you will be rewarded. These blessings are good evidence that you have found your gift.

Something additional to keep in mind: God gave Paul a "thorn in the flesh" (2 Corinthians 12:7), which Paul wanted taken away. But God revealed to him the thorn was for his good, to keep him humble so the power of Christ would dwell in him. Paul decided to glory in and even take pleasure in the thorn. Whatever your gift(s) is, you are responsible for using it (them) according to His plan.

FAITHFULNESS IN THE USE OF YOUR GIFT(S) IS THE KEY TO ETERNAL SUCCESS.

I remember a man named Floyd who served his church faithfully as a deacon, Sunday School director, and music director.

As he grew older, younger people were chosen for those notable works. He still had a love for people and a warm way of greeting them. He decided he would help others feel wanted and welcomed when they came to worship. It was not a commanding position but, as Jesus said, the one who serves becomes the greatest. For several years at the end of his life, he welcomed people who came to church.

At his funeral, when they celebrated Floyd's departure to glory, the building was packed. The pastor preached from Romans 8, Floyd's favorite passage. Some were saved as a result. Gifts may not appear as we think they should. Toward the end of his life, it looked like Floyd's gifts were diminishing, but they were actually expanding in a different direction.

Stewardship of abilities begins with thankful acceptance of the abilities God has given you. It continues with the discovery of what these abilities are and the faithful use of them within your local church body for the purposes of God. In the process, other abilities may become yours and your ministry will expand. Stewardship ends in that awesome moment when we stand before Christ, accountable to Him—not before.

As Solomon the wise man wrote: "Whatever your hand finds to do, do it with all your might" (Ecclesiastes 9:10).

REFLECTIONS

1. Write a brief statement describing your perception of the difference between common and uncommon abilities.

2. No doubt you have written a thank you note to a friend for a

gift. In a similar way, write a thank you note to God for every ability (common and uncommon) He has given you.

3. Write out a plan for putting your "body gifts" into service in your church. Share this with your pastor.

CHAPTER 5

BE FAITHFUL WITH YOUR TIME

There is a time for everything, and a season for every activity under the heavens: a time to be born and a time to die, a time to plant and a time to uproot, a time to kill and a time to heal, a time to tear down and a time to build, a time to weep and a time to laugh, a time to mourn and a time to dance, a time to scatter stones and a time to gather them, a time to embrace and a time to refrain from embracing, a time to search and a time to give up, a time to keep and a time to throw away, a time to tear and a time to mend, a time to be silent and a time to speak, a time to love and a time to hate, a time for war and a time for peace.

—ECCLESIASTES 3:1–8

See then that you walk circumspectly, not as fools but as wise, redeeming the time, because the days are evil. Therefore do not be unwise, but understand what the will of the Lord is.

—EPHESIANS 5:15–17 NKJV

Be still before the LORD and wait patiently for him;
do not fret when people succeed in their ways,
when they carry out their wicked schemes.

—PSALM 37:7

Are you going somewhere or just traveling? Time provides the opportunity to "go somewhere" with life. Wise stewardship of time is traveling to the right somewhere. Wisdom in time stewardship is redeeming time, conducting life according to the will of God.

To help you gain the perspective that time is important in your spiritual life, consider that the Bible includes many passages that mention time. Here are just a few examples: Acts 1:6; 3:21; 14:3; Romans 3:26; 13:11; 2 Corinthians 6:2; Galatians 4:4; 6:9; Ephesians 5:16; 1 Timothy 6:13–16; Hebrews 4:7; 1 Peter 1:10–12; 5:6–7.

Let me ask a question: do all of us have the same amount of time? The answer is both yes and no. Yes, if *amount* means each of us has 60 seconds per minute, 60 minutes per hour, and 24 hours per day. No, if *amount* means time that is available for our personal use. For example, when a couple chooses to become parents, they change the number of hours available for their personal use. Furthermore, we do not all live the same number of years, so we each manage a unique amount of seconds, minutes, days, months, and years in our lifetime. Each of us is a steward of how we manage our time allotment.

REDEEMING TIME IS OUR GRAND
STEWARDSHIP OPPORTUNITY!

The King James Version of Ephesians 5:16 records time stewardship as "redeeming the time." Redeeming here means, "paying a price to recover from the power of another." Wise use of time is not automatic. To redeem time, we must pay a price, expend effort, set priorities, and make plans. Otherwise we become a servant of the clock and the calendar, and the evil times in which we live will set our agenda. To let time slip by unredeemed is to let life slip by unredeemed.

"The days are evil" (Ephesians 5:16 KJV). We can and must make the effort to establish an agenda to redeem the time. Evil means "full of labors, annoyances, hardships, perils, sin, and wrongdoing." All of these characteristics of evil come naturally and automatically in life.

The world's agenda is evil. Sinning is often treated as an accomplishment these days. For example, many people simply endure the week so they can have another sin-filled weekend. People entertain themselves with sex, lust, and violence. Merchants use those same vices to sell everything from cars to toys. Greed corrupts our values. Unresolved hatred and guilt destroy our peace of mind. Addiction to alcohol, drugs, and work robs us of a quality life. Success, by the world's definition, is wealth, position, power, and popularity. Jesus said we are "sheep in the midst of wolves" (Matthew 10:16 NASB). If we simply take whatever agenda the times hand us, the result will be evil.

The tense of the verb *redeem* suggests that we redeem the time for ourselves. No one else can redeem time for me or for you. Whatever others do, whatever others suggest, we must redeem our time from evil and manage it ourselves. Other people will set the agenda for us if we do not have an agenda of our own.

There is a promise in the challenge of Ephesians 5:16. It says we can win over the evil; we can change the pattern; we can redeem the opportunity and seize the moment. We can even influence our times toward Christ!

WE WILL GIVE AN ACCOUNT TO OUR LORD FOR OUR STEWARDSHIP OF TIME.

The day of judgment has been appointed (Acts 17:31). Wise advice is given us in Romans 13:12–14:

> The night is nearly over; the day is almost here. So let us put aside the deeds of darkness and put on the armor of light. Let us behave decently, as in the daytime, not in carousing and drunkenness, not in sexual immorality and debauchery, not in dissension and jealousy. Rather, clothe yourselves with the Lord Jesus Christ, and do not think about how to gratify the desires of the flesh.

Establishing godly priorities and setting healthy boundaries are essential to good stewardship of time.

The Bible speaks of discerning excellent priorities (Philippians 1:10). It is easier to choose inferior priorities than it is to choose excellent priorities. To choose excellent priorities we must take two basic actions. First, consider what areas of our life need priority time, energy, and resources. Include family, church, vocation, and personal growth (spiritual, mental, social, and physical).

Next, establish the proper balance of time, energy, and resources for each priority. For example, in the area of family, priority should be given to the marriage relationship, relating to each child, and managing the family finances. This establishment of priorities will not be accomplished overnight and must stay amendable as the needs of life change.

It is impossible to establish excellent priorities without God's help. We are too blind or nearsighted and too short of understanding to do it alone. But here is the good news: God is interested in helping us do this. He will give wisdom to anyone who asks in faith (James 1:5–8). Good use of time will emerge from following good priorities.

REDEEMING TIME INVOLVES DOING THE RIGHT THING AT THE RIGHT TIME.

The time management focus of the world is on efficiency. We make lists, budget time, organize, schedule, and plan to keep from wasting a single moment. Time management books and seminars abound and some can be helpful to a committed steward.

However, you can use time efficiently by the world's standards and still not manage your time well. It is possible to climb the ladder to success efficiently, only to discover that it is leaning against the wrong wall. The Bible emphasizes choosing to lean your ladder against the "right" wall. Taking the right action at the right time in pursuit of the right priorities is good time stewardship. The issue is not doing things right, but doing the right things.

DOING THE RIGHT THING AT THE RIGHT TIME IS POSSIBLE ONLY IF WE UNDERSTAND AND DO THE WILL OF GOD.

God alone is wise enough to know what the right thing is. He knows the demands of today and tomorrow. God knows your potential. He knows how to lead you from where you are to where you need to go. God cares; He loves you more than all others who ask for your time. You can trust Him, the one who gave His only Son to save you, to lead you in the right way and to the right destination.

None of us naturally understand the will of God. The strongest obstacle to understanding God's will is our humanistic desire to set our own agenda and do our own will. Understanding God's will includes discarding our agenda and wholeheartedly accepting His agenda.

GOD FREELY REVEALS HIS WILL IN HIS WORD, THE BIBLE.

The Ten Commandments state His will. The Sermon on the Mount states His will. Many passages say outright, "This is God's will." For example, we know it is God's will to deliver us from the evil of this present world because the Bible says Christ "gave himself for our sins to rescue us from the present evil age, according to the will of our God and Father" (Galatians 1:4).

What are other examples of God's stated will?

- Ephesians 6:6—Work with integrity and dependability.
- 1 Thessalonians 4:3—Abstain from sexual fornication.

- 1 Thessalonians 5:16–18—Rejoice always, pray continually, and give thanks in everything.
- 1 Peter 2:13–15—Be a good, law-abiding citizen.
- 1 Peter 3:17 and 4:19—Do good, even if that means you will suffer.
- Ephesians 5:21–33—Seek a strong and fulfilling marriage, and become one with your spouse.
- Ephesians 6:1–4—Be an effective parent and obedient child.
- 1 Timothy 5:8—Provide for the material, emotional, physical, and spiritual needs of your family.
- Romans 13:6–8—Conduct business honestly, and never incur debt beyond your ability to pay.

Other Scriptures state that praying, worshiping, giving, witnessing, and exercising our spiritual gifts are all God's will.

God's purposes for us also reveal His will. For example, it is God's purpose that we become like Christ. "For those God foreknew he also predestined to be conformed to the image of his Son, that he might be the firstborn among many brothers and sisters" (Romans 8:29; see also Ephesians 4:15).

Good stewardship of time includes provision for growing into Christlikeness. Christ was a perfect time manager, always doing the right thing at the right time (John 7:6, 8). Consider some examples: He was born at the right time (Galatians 4:4); He began preaching at the right time (Mark 1:15); and He went to Jerusalem and was betrayed and crucified at the right time (Mark 14:41).

God has declared that there is a time for everything.
Being in time with God's will is more important than being on time. A sewing machine is a good example of the importance

of being in time. The working parts of the machine must move precisely in time with each other for the stitching to be correct. If the machine gets out of time, the stitching will not be right despite the intentions and efforts of the sewing machine operator. So, if we are not in time with God's will, life will not turn out right, no matter our effort and intentions.

God's Spirit, who dwells within us, reveals His will to us. Jesus said that the Spirit will guide us into all truth, teach us all things, and remind us of what Jesus said (John 14:26; 16:13). We also read that the Spirit prays for us "in accordance with the will of God" (Romans 8:27). He can guide us to know what the will of God is in any circumstance. The Spirit abides within us to help us do God's will, "for it is God who works in you to will and to act in order to fulfill his good purpose" (Philippians 2:13). Knowing this, we can use our time to the maximum efficiency.

Paul conducted his life by the will of God as revealed in the Bible and by the Holy Spirit. His vocational choice and the epistles he penned were by the will of God. On his second missionary journey he tried to go to Asia, but the Holy Spirit forbade it. He then tried to go to Bithynia, but the Spirit did not allow it. So he went forward to Troas where God revealed to him that he should go to Macedonia (Acts 16:6–10). He learned to only go where God directed him.

God's will is that we do what He reveals as important, not what others say is urgent.

Again, our example is Jesus. We read in Mark 1 that as He ministered in Capernaum, people gathered around Him, sought Him, listened to Him, and requested His ministry. It was late that night when Jesus healed the last sick person. Early the next morning, before daylight, Jesus arose from His bed and slipped out of town to a private place to pray.

When the city awoke, people came to the house for Jesus again. Simon and the disciples searched for Him, and when they found Him they reminded Him that everyone was looking for Him (v. 37). Instead of responding to the urging of the disciples and the people, Jesus went to a nearby town to minister. He chose to do the important rather than the urgent.

Good stewardship of time begins with understanding and doing the will of God. It touches every area of life: home, marriage, sex, parent-child relationships, finances, food, clothing, debt, savings, vocation, recreation, church, and worship.

Good stewardship of time will keep us from being bound to a stressful schedule.

Over-involvement is not good stewardship. Rest is an essential part of good time management. God rested and set aside one day each week for rest and worship (Exodus 20:8–11). God put three weeks into the Old Testament calendar for everyone to stop working and celebrate (Exodus 12; 23:14–19). Every seventh and fiftieth year were to be different in work demands and celebration (Leviticus 25). God will never cause us to burn out doing His will. He has special refreshment and strength for those who wait on Him. To wait means looking to God expectantly, fully assured that doing His will is primary and that God will empower us to do it. God's Spirit is the source of our strength and bears wonderful fruit in us: "love, joy, peace, forbearance, kindness, goodness, faithfulness, gentleness and self-control" (Galatians 5:22–23).

THE BIBLE GIVES US SOME EXCELLENT TIME REMINDERS.

The Bible gives us daily reminders: morning, noon, and evening are times for seeking God in prayer, in meditation, in His Word, and in worship (see Psalm 5:3; 55:17; 59:16; 88:13; 119:147; 143:8). It marks sundown as the deadline for being angry. The sun is not to go down on our wrath or exasperation (Ephesians 4:26).

The Bible gives us weekly and seasonal reminders. Sunday, the first day of the week, is the time for gathering with our fellow believers in worship and giving (1 Corinthians 16:2). A major purpose for gathering together for worship is to encourage one another and "stimulate one another to love and good deeds" (Hebrews 10:24 NASB). All of us need encouragement and motivation. We gather to be encouraged and motivated, but we also come together as a body of believers to encourage and stimulate each other. This is good stewardship of time.

"Six days you shall labor and do all your work" (Exodus 20:9 NKJV). This verse is a clear reminder about stewardship of time. Work is a good use of time, and laziness is a poor use of time. Proverbs 6:6 admonishes the lazy person to learn from the lowly ant. The ant works at the opportune time. That is the key—not how hard or how long you work but how well you work at the right time.

In 2 Thessalonians 3:10 we read that those who refuse to work should not receive free food. Choosing the right occupation is a vital part of your time stewardship, but how you work and why you work is more important than where you work. In the New Testament days, slaves (who certainly did not choose their occupation) were admonished to work honestly, sincerely, and faithfully as though Jesus was their boss (Ephesians 6:5–8).

Working with that attitude can make any job holy. It does the will of God as well as earns the pay of men—and the reward of Christ.

Our lives are fleeting.
We know how many hours are in a day and how many days are in a week, but we do not know how much time we ultimately have to manage. At any moment an accident or illness could change or end our lives. Life is fragile, and we can be called to give account to our Lord at any moment. It is a relief to know that God, who knows all, will guide us as we seek to be good stewards. Moses wrote in Psalm 90:12: "Teach us to number our days, that we may gain a heart of wisdom."

Jesus is our perfect example of how to manage time.
He always did the right thing at the right time. He did every-thing He was supposed to do in His life and ministry. In His high-priestly prayer He said, "I have finished the work which You have given Me to do" (John 17:4 NKJV). Jesus never let anyone but His Father set His agenda, though many tried. He said, "I can of Myself do nothing. . . . because I do not seek My own will but the will of the Father who sent Me" (John 5:30 NKJV). When He faced Crucifixion, He prayed to the Father, "not my will, but Yours, be done" (Luke 22:42 NKJV). And after paying for our sin on the Cross He said, "It is finished" (John 19:30).

Jesus was the most successful person who ever lived. He had time for the multitudes and time for the individual. He stopped in the midst of a crowd to give blind Bartimaeus sight (Mark 10:46–52). Remember, although Jesus lived in a time when there were none of the modern conveniences or communication devices we have, He was no less busy than anyone today.

So, how do we manage our time, the time God gives us each day? Some people use a written schedule. Others keep their schedules on their computer or phone. Whatever method you use to manage your schedule, never let your schedule replace the dynamic will of God as His Spirit applies His Word to you!

REFLECTIONS

1. Name as many of the Bible's definitions of time as you can.

2. Do you think everyone has the same amount of time? Explain your answer.

3. Why must a good steward redeem time? How can a good steward redeem time?

4. List characteristics of a good time manager based on biblical principles.

CHAPTER 6

BE FAITHFUL IN YOUR RELATIONSHIPS

Submit to one another out of reverence for Christ. Wives, submit yourselves to your own husbands as you do to the Lord. . . . Husbands, love your wives, just as Christ loved the church and gave himself up for her to make her holy. . . . In this same way, husbands ought to love their wives as their own bodies. He who loves his wife loves himself. . . . However, each one of you also must love his wife as he loves himself, and the wife must respect her husband.

—EPHESIANS 5:21–22, 25–26, 28, 33

Children, obey your parents in the Lord, for this is right. "Honor your father and mother"—which is the first commandment with a promise—"so that it may go well with you and that you may enjoy long life on the earth." Fathers, do not exasperate your children; instead, bring them up in the training and instruction of the Lord.

—EPHESIANS 6:1–4

L ife and relationships are almost synonymous. We are all part of a network of relationships. We have relationships with people from our family, friends, church, workplace, neighborhood, community, state, and nation. Our relationships trace back to Adam and extend to all the people on earth. Moreover, that network of relationships will exist forever. Wow! How heavy can it get?

We are simultaneously blessed, challenged, and sometimes wounded by our relationships. God revealed this very early in Genesis by recording the first murder, which happened in the first family on earth. Cain intentionally killed his brother, Abel, and the Lord said to Cain:

> *"Where is your brother Abel?"*
>
> *"I don't know," he replied. "Am I my brother's keeper?"*
>
> *The Lord said, "What have you done? Listen! Your brother's blood cries out to me from the ground."*
> —GENESIS 4:9–10

Despite the possibility of being wounded by our relationships, we are accountable to some of the people around us. And we are ultimately all accountable to God. We are stewards of all our relationships past, present, and future, our family relationships, our civic relationships, and our church relationships.

WE ARE STEWARDS OF OUR HERITAGE: PAST, PRESENT, AND FUTURE.

We are greatly influenced by all that has gone on before us. We owe a debt to all from whom we have inherited benefits. Many advantages afforded citizens of the United States came from the hard work and unselfish sacrifice of other people. Through a network of trade that we did not establish, the food we eat each day comes to our table from all over the world. The Bible is available in a language we can read because of people like John Wycliffe and others who were killed for their courageous translation efforts. Before them were the Hebrew people God chose to receive and record His revelation of Himself. Included in their number are those early Christians through whom God gave us the New Covenant. When Paul preached to the Gentiles, he preached to people many of us call ancestors, people who were pagans, worshiping false gods and demons.

This debt calls for payment by passing on the faith once delivered to the saints to generations to come. Scripture says it best: "Therefore, since we are surrounded by such a great cloud of witnesses, let us throw off everything that hinders and the sin that so easily entangles. And let us run with perseverance the race marked out for us, fixing our eyes on Jesus, the pioneer and perfecter of faith. For the joy set before him he endured the cross, scorning its shame, and sat down at the right hand of the throne of God" (Hebrews 12:1–2).

We owe a debt to those who have come before us; I pray for God to enable us to be faithful to pass along what we've been graciously granted. And I hope the generations who come after us will benefit from that God-empowered faithfulness.

As strange as it may sound, we also have a stewardship responsibility to deal properly with all of the bad influence that is handed to us. A pastor friend told me about a young couple he recently united in marriage. Before they came to know Christ, they lived together while unmarried. In their serious efforts to follow Christ, they decided they should be married. They also showed integrity in other relationships. Their work and daily lifestyle reflected their loyalty to Christ. All of this is in contrast to their family backgrounds. His father was married four times and had several children by a variety of women. Her mother, who was in prison when the story unfolded, was similarly married several times with several children by those marriages. The young people were following their bad heritage—all they had known—until they met Christ. In His power, they interrupted that destructive cycle.

Many people find it necessary to seek Bible-based Christian counseling in their struggle to deal in a redemptive way with the scars of their past. It is easy to blame those who wound us, but blaming never solves the problem. We are not responsible for what they did to us; we are responsible for how we react. Our reaction shapes the quality of our life and what we pass on to those who come after us.

WE ARE STEWARDS OF FAMILY RELATIONSHIPS.

The Bible has a lot to say about family relationships. Much of the book of Genesis is family stories. Sometimes family relationships are healthy; sometimes they are dysfunctional. The Bible tells it like it is.

Many passages contain commands and wise counsel for family matters. Two of the Ten Commandments deal directly with family issues, specifically parent-child and husband-wife relationships. "Honor your father and your mother, so that you may live long in the land the LORD your God is giving you. You shall not commit adultery" (Exodus 20:12, 14).

Husband-wife relationships are dealt with extensively throughout Scripture. The excellent (virtuous) wife described in Proverbs 31:10–31 is worth more than jewels. She is trustworthy and does her husband good all her life. She is industrious in providing for her family. Active in business outside the home, she works for her family's benefit. She is a loving person who helps the poor. The way she dresses is an asset to her husband. She uses her mind to gain wisdom and discreetly passes it on. Her inner beauty is more important than her natural physical beauty. She has a strong and deep relationship with God, and her family praises her.

A key passage on marriage is found in Ephesians 5:21–33. The beginning statement, which is often overlooked, is, "Submit to one another out of reverence for Christ" (v. 21). As stewards of the marriage relationship, each partner, both husband and wife, submits to meeting the other's needs. Each lives to make the other happy. According to *Thayer's Greek–English Lexicon*, the word translated *submit* in Ephesians 5:21 means "a voluntary attitude of giving in, cooperating, assuming responsibility, carrying a burden." Friendships call for some "giving in." Even more so, the marriage relationship calls for cooperating or assuming responsibility. Marriage is compared to Christ's love for the church, which took Him to His death on the Cross. Submission, properly understood, is a key element in developing a successful marriage.

Parent-child relationships also get top priority in God's Word. The annual Passover Feast was a family affair; its message was to be explained to the children (Exodus 12:26). The Ten Commandments affirm that both the sins of wicked parents and the love and obedience of righteous parents affect children for generations to come (20:5–6). Parents, especially fathers, are commanded to live by God's Word and teach it to their children so they may have a long and good life (Deuteronomy 6:6–9, 18–21).

Parenting is a very serious issue. Malachi said the preaching of a future prophet (John the Baptist) "will turn the hearts of the parents to their children, and the hearts of the children to their parents; or else I will come and strike the land with total destruction" (Malachi 4:6). Our relationship with God is presented as a father-child relationship: "As a father has compassion on his children, so the Lord has compassion on those who fear him" (Psalm 103:13) and, "the Lord disciplines those he loves, as a father the son he delights in" (Proverbs 3:12). These are only a few typical examples.

The Bible takes the attitude that "children *are* a heritage from the Lord, the fruit of the womb *is* a reward. Like arrows are in the hand of a warrior, so *are* the children of one's youth. Happy *is* the man who has his quiver full of them" (Psalm 127:3–5 NKJV). When God gives us children, He puts a priceless trust in our hands. Parents are stewards of that trust.

Parents find many examples in the Bible, good and bad, to help them in their stewardship. Both Jacob and Eli provide bad examples. Jacob's favoritism for Joseph caused many problems in his family. The priest Eli's failure to properly discipline his sons caused Eli great sorrow and brought a curse on the family line (1 Samuel 2:12–17, 27–34).

The Bible also provides positive examples. Hannah's unselfish love for her son Samuel as she devoted him to the service of the Lord was a strong influence in his rise to greatness (1 Samuel 1–3). The Philippian jailor's conversion to Christ became the key to the salvation of his entire family (Acts 16:31–34). One of the best examples of providing a legacy of faith is the grandmother and mother of Timothy. He caught their contagious faith and shone like a star in the New Testament (2 Timothy 1:5).

An excellent passage on the parent-child relationship is Ephesians 6:1–4. Children are reminded that they are to honor and obey their parents. God promises a long and good life to such children. Parents, especially fathers, are commanded not to provoke their children to the point of exasperation or discouragement but to "bring them up in the training and instruction of the Lord" (v. 4). These are short statements that leave great latitude for interpretation as to exactly what the training includes. In this, as in all else, we need to seek wisdom from God.

A God-centered family (husband-wife and parent-child) relationship is the cornerstone of excellence in human civilization. This is a primary stewardship!

SOCIAL RELATIONSHIPS ARE IMPORTANT.

Christ said we are to be in the world but not of the world (John 17:16–17). Six of the Ten Commandments address our social relationships. We have stewardship responsibilities toward our friends, our neighbors, our community, the people we chance to meet, the people we have never met, and our government (city, county, state, and federal). In all these relationships we are responsible for being salt and light. More than just not causing harm, we are to be a positive force for good and for God.

Jesus affirmed that the second greatest commandment is to love your neighbor as yourself (Matthew 22:34–40, Luke 10:27). Referring to the second greatest commandment, a man once asked Jesus, "Who is my neighbor?" Jesus replied with the story of the Good Samaritan (Luke 10:25–37). The answer to the question is this: your neighbor is the person in need, whether known or unknown, whether in your social class or not. Most people seem to know very little about the neighbors who live near them. If you believe God is in charge of your life, then you must acknowledge that your set of neighbors is no accident. They are your field for sowing seed, watering, cultivating, and harvesting.

If you were unsaved, how would you want your saved neighbor to treat you? The Golden Rule works very well here! Are your neighbors lonely, sad, depressed, grieving? Are some lost, addicted, or bound by some destructive sin? God has given you your neighbors; be salt and light.

We are stewards of our relationship to our government. Jesus said "Give back to Caesar what is Caesar's, and to God what is God's" (Matthew 22:21). In our system of government we are responsible for everything from voting to running for political office. We are to pay our taxes, show respect for those in office, and obey the laws (Romans 13:1). We are to pray for our government leaders, especially that they will be saved (1 Timothy 2:1–4). The Bible shows us that God is gracious to hear the humble prayers of His people. So, let's pray for our country and trust God to hear and answer in accordance with His will (2 Chronicles 7:14).

FAITHFUL STEWARDSHIP OF CHURCH RELATIONSHIPS PRODUCES GOOD FRUIT.

Faithfulness calls for us to join a church soon after we receive Christ as Savior, become a participating member of the body we have joined, maintain a love relationship with our fellow church members, and play a vital role on a team that is assigned the task of making disciples of all nations.

If the words *joining* and *member* are problems for you, find out what the Bible really says on this subject. You won't find many direct commands, but you will find some assumptions and examples. Jesus assumed that His followers would be a part of a local body of believers when He gave the prescription for handling fellowship problems in Matthew 18:15–17. He said the third step in seeking reconciliation is "tell it to the church" (v. 17). If you are not a member of a local church, how can you obey that command?

Look at two examples of people becoming members. First, baptized believers on the day of Pentecost were added to the church, or the body of believers gathered together (Acts 2:47). According to *Thayer's Greek–English Lexicon*, the Greek word for church in that verse is *ekklesia*, and it means the "called out ones" or the "called together" ones. That word is translated throughout the New Testament as "church."

Second, when Paul first attended the church at Jerusalem after his conversion, the Bible says that he tried to join the disciples (Acts 9:26). The Greek word translated "join" is *kollaw*. According to the *NAS New Testament Greek Lexicon*, it means to "glue together." That is what happens when you join a church. You and they have a sense of belonging that does not come with simply "fellowshipping." Add to that the fact that the word *parts* is used several times in 1 Corinthians 12 to refer precisely to belonging to a local body of believers. The metaphor is that of a human body. Its parts are firmly attached and committed to the body. Joining a local body of believers (church) is the right thing to do.

Joining is just the beginning of an active participating relationship. Every member (or "part") has at least one spiritual gift for making the church body whole (1 Corinthians 12:12–14). For a human body to function properly, each member of the body must be attached, active, and working in harmony with the rest of the body. The simple task of eating requires the cooperation of many parts of the body: the nervous system, the fingers, hands, wrists, arms, shoulders, eyes, mouth, teeth, tongue, and much more. So it is with a church.

Fellowship with other members must be maintained. It is normal for fellowship problems to arise. The scriptural record contains several reports of fellowship problems among the 12 apostles. Fellowship problems surfaced throughout the New Testament. Jesus gave us instructions for reconciling with one another (Matthew 5:23–24; 18:15–17).

For some strange reason we continue to be surprised by fellowship problems. Churches are made up of people, and where there are people there will be problems. Good stewardship calls for us to seek reconciliation promptly. Some key statements in reconciling are: "I was wrong," "I am sorry," "I ask you to forgive me," "I forgive you." Those words must be said clearly and with feeling and integrity. Some people are afraid to forgive. Perhaps some do not understand that forgiveness means, "I release the debt. I won't try to make you pay any more." Forgiving does not mean you are saying, "What you did was OK," or "You are free to do it again." When we confess our sins to God He forgives, but He never says, "What you did was OK," or "You are free to do it again." He simply does not hold it against us any longer; He releases the debt.

Forgiveness opens the door to reconciliation, but reconciliation and forgiveness are not the same. You can and must release the debt you hold against another person. But you may find that person is not willing to be reconciled. Or, although forgiveness is necessary on your part, there are times when it is not wise or safe to continue in a relationship with the other person.

Confronting a fellow believer is never easy. It can only be done effectively in the power of the Holy Spirit. Since God commands it, you can count on Him to help you do it. Your motive must be reconciliation. Getting even, manipulating, or playing power games must never be your intent. Actually, confronting a person with the intention of reconciliation is a compliment. It says, "This relationship is important to me and I want to patch it up."

OUR MOST IMPORTANT RELATIONSHIP IS WITH GOD.

Our relationship with God is established when we repent of our sins and believe on the Lord Jesus Christ as Savior. Then God calls us "into fellowship with his Son" (1 Corinthians 1:9). It is awesome to think that we can have fellowship with the same Jesus who fellowshipped with Peter, James, and John.

Our relationship to God is by spiritual birth, and it never changes. But our fellowship with God is constantly fluctuating.

Fellowship rises and falls in direct proportion to our obedience. Sin breaks our fellowship. Anything that breaks our fellowship with Christ is a sin, whether the action alone is considered a sin or not. The Bible says, "If we claim to have fellowship with him and yet walk in the darkness, we lie and do not live out the truth. But if we walk in the light, as he is in the light, we have fellowship with one another, and the blood of Jesus, his Son, purifies us from all sin" (1 John 1:6–7). Walking in the light, "as he is in the light," is the key to fellowship. When we break the fellowship, God wants to restore it and be reconciled. He made it very simple and spelled it out for us. "If we confess our sins, he is faithful and just and will forgive us our sins and purify us from all unrighteousness" (1 John 1:9).

Good stewardship of relationships includes establishing, cultivating, and maintaining them. The people in our neighborhood need good relationships. Our families need good relationships. Our churches need good relationships. Our nation needs good relationships. We are the only ones who can meet these needs through the power of Christ.

REFLECTIONS

1. Identify at least two negative and two positive impacts your personal heritage has made on you. Write a brief statement describing how you will be a good steward of all four.

2. Identify some ways you can develop better relationships

   - in your marriage
   - in your parent-child relationships

- with your friends
- with your enemies
- with your neighbors
- with your church

3. What definite things can you do to pass on a good heritage to those who come after you?

4. Write some ways you have been blessed by a word or deed from someone else. Make plans to pass a similar blessing on to someone else today.

CHAPTER 7

BE FAITHFUL WITH YOUR SUBSTANCE

But remember the LORD your God, for it is he who gives you the ability to produce wealth, and so confirms his covenant, which he swore to your ancestors, as it is today.

—DEUTERONOMY 8:18

"Will a mere mortal rob God? Yet you rob me. But you ask, 'How are we robbing you?' In tithes and offerings. . . . Bring the whole tithe into the storehouse, that there may be food in my house. Test me in this," says the LORD Almighty, "and see if I will not throw open the floodgates of heaven and pour out so much blessing that there will not be room enough to store it. Then all the nations will call you blessed, for yours will be a delightful land," says the LORD Almighty.

—MALACHI 3:8, 10, 12

Give, and it will be given to you. A good measure, pressed down, shaken together and running over,

*will be poured into your lap. For with the measure
you use, it will be measured to you.*

—LUKE 6:38

*Remember this: Whoever sows sparingly will also
reap sparingly, and whoever sows generously will
also reap generously. Each of you should give what
you have decided in your heart to give, not reluc-
tantly or under compulsion, for God loves a cheerful giver. . . . Now he who supplies seed to the sower
and bread for food will also supply and increase
your store of seed and will enlarge the harvest of
your righteousness. You will be enriched in every
way so that you can be generous on every occa-
sion, and through us your generosity will result in
thanksgiving to God.*

—2 CORINTHIANS 9:6–7, 10–11

In the King James Version, Proverbs 3:9–10 says: "Hon-
our the LORD with thy substance, and with the firstfruits
of all thine increase: so shall thy barns be filled with
plenty, and thy presses shall burst out with new wine."
For today's reader this quote brings up a lot of questions. First,
what is substance? How much of our substance are we to use
for God's honor? Why should we honor the Lord with our substance? How do we honor the Lord with our substance? What
is the result of honoring the Lord with our substance? Let's
answer these questions.

WHAT IS *SUBSTANCE*?

Although a word we don't use much today, *substance* covers "more than money": it covers all our possessions, from the barest necessities to lavish wealth. The Hebrew word for substance means wealth, but wealth is certainly a relative term. At times the Hebrew word means material possessions. Job used it for anything accrued since his birth (Job 1:21). The bottom line: every material thing we have is a trust from God and an excellent resource for doing great things.

Unfortunately, we tend to feel that "wealth" is always more than we happen to have. However, Merriam Webster's definition for wealth includes all material objects that have economic utility. Notice that ownership is established by "thy." It is true that everything belongs to God, but He has granted the right of possession to us in this life. The right of personal possession is recognized in the commandment, "You shall not steal" (Exodus 20:15 NKJV). Our inner feelings about personal possession are formed during the first few years of life. Practically speaking, I cannot personally honor God with my possessions unless they actually belong to me. So, substance is any personal possession.

HOW MUCH OF OUR SUBSTANCE ARE WE TO USE FOR GOD'S HONOR?

All of it, of course, 100 percent. It seems easier to think of honoring God with a tithe, or 10 percent of what we have, and using the rest of it any way we want. To honor Him with some, and not with all, puts us into the Pharisee/hypocrite category. Though they tithed meticulously—even to the smallest of spices—Jesus called them on their hypocrisy (Mark 7:10–13). All we have comes from His provision, and we are accountable to Him for all of it. That's stewardship.

TWO REASONS WE SHOULD HONOR GOD WITH OUR SUBSTANCE.

First, God deserves to be honored simply because He has supplied all of our substance. When someone makes a significant gift to a college, that person is usually honored in some special way. A library may be named after the donor, or there may be a public recognition ceremony. Many colleges bear the name of the person who made their existence possible.

I heard of a man who had some rental houses. His widowed mother lived in one of them and paid him rent from her very limited income. When inflation raised the price of rentals, he demanded higher rent from his mother. She truly could not afford it and pleaded with him to have mercy. Surely he could have compassion on the mother who gave him birth and kept him alive with her tender care through his helpless years. Not him. He had her evicted! We react with horror to such action. Why, then, do we have difficulty with the thought that we should honor God with all our substance? We seem to find it easy to forget it comes from Him.

God reminded Israel of the danger of forgetfulness as they approached the Promised Land (Deuteronomy 8:11–20). He identified four dangers of prosperity: a proud heart, forgetting God, taking credit for their prosperity, and turning to other gods. God reminded them that He is the One who gives the power to make wealth.

The power to make wealth does not reside in us. This is evident by the fact that many skilled, educated people work hard but live in poverty. Forgetting God's blessings can lead directly to ruin. Israel fell into forgetfulness and experienced ruin.

Other people need to see that Christians love God enough to honor Him with their substance. Our possessions provide us with that wonderful opportunity. Nothing reveals our true nature better than the way we use our possessions, including our money.

The idea of honoring God runs counter to the non-Christian worldview of managing possessions. The world's system is based on getting; God's system is based on giving. God is a giver! He gave life to every living creature. He gave Eve to Adam and Adam to Eve. He gave them dominion over the earth. "He himself gives everyone life and breath and everything else" (Acts 17:25). He gave His only begotten Son so we would not perish but have everlasting life (John 3:16). Jesus gave His life on the Cross for our sins. Salvation is a gift from God (Ephesians 2:8–9). When Christians honor God by giving their possessions to Him and managing them according to God's plan, they reflect a likeness to God.

What is the base of your economic plan—getting or giving? Getting easily turns to greed. In these times of easy credit, the getting mentality can quickly lead to excessive debt and oppressive payments. Everyone suffers when this happens: the debtor, the marriage, and the family. Problems compound, stress increases, depression sets in, and life loses its joy. Getting is basically selfish and is interested in pleasing self, not in honoring God.

Giving, on the other hand, develops in us a likeness to God, who is a giver by nature. It is in the system of giving that God meets all our needs. Parents give care, clothing, shelter, and security to their children. The children give honor to their parents. Parents give their children freedom to become the adults God wants them to be. The company gives the parents a job. The parents give the company their skills, time, and effort as if they were working for Christ. We give our life to Christ, and He gives us eternal life with Him. On and on the giving cycle goes, and more giving generates more blessing.

HOW CAN WE HONOR GOD WITH OUR SUBSTANCE?

We honor God by making and using our substance in obedience to His plan for our stewardship of possessions, which is clearly stated in the Bible.

We honor God by making money and gaining possessions in honorable ways. A Christian is out of place in an occupation that contributes to addictions, moral perversion, loss of values, damage to family life, mental confusion, or is otherwise damaging. Stealing, of any sort, is not honorable. Gambling is a form of stealing; winning greedily takes what belonged to another without giving anything in its place. Proverbs 13:11 tells us that, "Dishonest money dwindles away, but whoever gathers money little by little makes it grow." The mandate to the Christian is to work with our hands at "what is good, so that he will have *something* to share with one who has need" (Ephesians 4:28 NASB). "Good" means the Christian's occupation should have a positive effect on others.

We honor God by enjoying the substance He has supplied to us. Does it surprise you that God wants us to enjoy what He has given us? Long ago through the prophet Jeremiah, God revealed that His plan for us includes prosperity, hope, and a bright future (Jeremiah 29:11). However, there are limits and boundaries about how to enjoy our substance. It is never to be done in a way that damages us or other people. We settle for less than God's best for us when we transfer our trust from Him to our possessions or turn our joy into selfish indulgence.

We honor God by using our substance to provide the necessities of life. Failing to provide for our own is a denial of the faith and makes us worse than unbelievers (1 Timothy 5:8). Providing for our own begins with the immediate family—father, mother, son, daughter, brother, sister—and can encompass our extended family. Providing includes the material necessities of life, the mental necessity of education, and the spiritual necessities. Jesus scolded some scribes and Pharisees for failing to provide for their needy parents by claiming their possessions were instead totally devoted to God (Mark 7:9–13).

We honor God by paying our debts with our substance. We must be very careful about making debts. In these times of credit cards, it is very easy to get into more debt than we can pay. We honor God by making the payments on time. Our witness is damaged if we are neglectful about paying our debts. The only unpaid debt we are allowed is the debt of love for one another (Romans 13:8).

We honor God by providing for the future with our substance (2 Corinthians 12:14). Proverbs 6:6–11 reminds us of the lowly ant who stores up food in the summer when it is available. That passage labels a person as lazy who refuses to use available substance to prepare for the lean times. In a dream, God told the Pharaoh of Egypt that he should use seven good harvest years to prepare for seven lean years (Genesis 41:1–39). However, Jesus commanded us to avoid being preoccupied with seeking provision for tomorrow (Matthew 6:25–34). Our focus is to be His kingdom and righteousness. He promised if we would seek first the kingdom (rule) of God, He would meet all of tomorrow's needs. It is possible that God's care for tomorrow could come in the form of a surplus today, as it did for Egypt. But Jesus warned us against treasuring material things in our hearts (Matthew 6:19–24). This addresses our *attitude* toward savings and insurance, not the wisdom of saving and buying insurance.

One October, while in Colorado hunting elk with my son, we saw a flock of sparrows eating the seeds leftover from summer. God's way of taking care of them was by growing a surplus of seeds during the summer. Good stewardship calls for properly managing our surplus. Jesus told the apostles to pick up what was left over after feeding the 5,000 so that nothing would be wasted (John 6:12). Both worry and wastefulness are poor stewardship. If God provides more than you need today, He either wants you to give it away or use it to provide for tomorrow. He can lead you to manage it well if you are putting Him first.

Providing for the future also includes laying up treasure in heaven (Matthew 6:19–21). First we must believe on the Lord Jesus Christ as our personal Savior. Then we must use the substance He provides for us to do eternal things.

We honor God when we give of our substance. Though this is really the first way we honor God with our substance, I mention it last so you see there are many ways to honor God with your possessions. Proverbs 3:9 calls for the "firstfruits," or giving to God first, before we do anything else with our possessions.

Her first name was May. Her husband left her with two small girls to raise. The only job May could get was working in a laundry. The pay was meager, hardly enough to meet their needs. One night she hosted a prayer meeting for the coming revival. When she opened her Bible to give the devotional, her Sunday School offering envelope fell out. She blushed a bit and explained that she always put her tithe in her Bible first so she wouldn't spend it for other things. God was first in her heart! God did meet May's needs and helped her raise two fine girls to adulthood.

Clearly the tithe (10 percent) belongs to the Lord (Leviticus 27:30). Nowhere in the Bible does He revoke the tithe. Malachi 3:9 informs us that using the tithe for ourselves will bring a curse. Are you aware that many Christians are living "under a curse" financially? If you want to know what it is like to live under that curse, read Haggai 1:5–10. People who are living under a curse often run out of money before needs are met, and they expect more than they receive. On the other hand, God promised a blessing to those who would bring the tithe into the storehouse (Malachi 3:8–12). The blessing extends to the nation. How many of our national economic problems are caused by people not tithing and not being good stewards of the rest of their possessions?

Christians, living under the New Covenant, should not stop with the tithe. The Christian's economic system is described in 2 Corinthians 9:6–15, as having six elements:

1. If you sow (give) bountifully, you will reap bountifully.
2. You are to be a cheerful, generous giver like God.

3. God will enable you to give generously.
4. God will increase the harvest of your righteousness.
5. The needs of others will be supplied.
6. Others will glorify God because of your giving.

What are the results of honoring God with our substance?

Proverbs 3:10 (NKJV) says, "So your barns will be filled with plenty, and your vats will overflow with new wine." Your needs, and those of your family, will be met. Your work will take on new meaning. Managing your possessions will become productive. Your church will have enough money to finance everything God leads it to do. Your witness to the unsaved will be more effective. You will enjoy a real fellowship with Christ in your daily life. All your possessions will take on a sacred meaning. And at the end you will hear the Lord say, "Well done."

REFLECTIONS

1. Make an inventory of the substance God has entrusted to you.

2. Clarify in your own mind and heart two reasons you should honor God with the substance that He has entrusted to you.

3. This chapter stated six ways to honor God with your substance. How many of them can you name without looking?

4. Can you think of other specific ways you can honor God with your substance?

CHAPTER 8

BE FAITHFUL IN YOUR POSITIONS

You also, like living stones, are being built into a spiritual house to be a holy priesthood, offering spiritual sacrifices acceptable to God through Jesus Christ. For in Scripture it says: "See, I lay a stone in Zion, a chosen and precious cornerstone, and the one who trusts in him will never be put to shame."

Now to you who believe, this stone is precious. But to those who do not believe, "The stone the builders rejected has become the cornerstone," and, "A stone that causes people to stumble and a rock that makes them fall." They stumble because they disobey the message—which is also what they were destined for.

But you are a chosen people, a royal priesthood, a holy nation, God's special possession, that you may declare the praises of him who called you out of darkness into his wonderful light. Once you were not a people, but now you are the people of God; once you had not received mercy, but now you have received mercy.

—1 PETER 2:5–10

We tend to forget that we have responsible positions that include being: parents, children, siblings, employees and/or employers, a child of God, an ambassador of Christ, even a sheep among wolves.

Our primary responsibility is to God, but we are also responsible to people who are affected by how we manage our positions.

A great position passage is found in 1 Peter 2:9–10. It identifies several positions of believers in the Lord Jesus Christ. We are: a chosen people, a royal priesthood, God's special possession, and a holy nation—the people of God.

Because our awesomely rich position in Christ defines who we are and our spiritual functions, we need to take two steps: acknowledge our position and accept our position.

ACKNOWLEDGE YOUR POSITION.

You are both a holy (v. 5) and a royal (v. 9) priest. The same God who instructed Samuel to anoint David as royal king of Israel has made you royalty. However, your priesthood is superior to the Old Testament priesthood. They were holy priests; you are both holy and royal.

Christ qualified you to be a priest through several spiritual actions: He chose you, He sanctified you through the work of the Spirit and the sprinkling of His blood, He caused you to be born again, and He saved you. You will find some of these elements in His choosing of the Old Testament priests.

You may say, "I don't feel like a priest." Let me ask you, "How does a priest feel?" You have been a priest since you were saved. Have you ever acknowledged it?

ACCEPT YOUR PRIESTHOOD.

It is possible to acknowledge the reality of being a priest yet reject the role. Accepting means you are willing to serve as a priest. But what does a New Testament priest do? In the past, the emphasis was almost exclusively on our right to approach God in prayer without any other human mediator. Though this is a valid application of our priesthood, it is only one facet.

Our focal passage in 1 Peter 2 assigns to us two positive actions that are wonderful. As a priest, we offer up "spiritual sacrifices acceptable to God by Jesus Christ" (v. 5). We also "proclaim the excellencies of Him who has called you out of darkness into His marvelous light" (v. 9 NASB). It will ignite your sense of purpose to examine each of these applications carefully.

We are to offer up spiritual sacrifices acceptable to God. We can offer the sacrifice of service in a way that God will accept and bless. We can offer our gifts of tithes and offerings, which God will accept and bless. We can give a thirsty person a cup of cold water, and God will bless it. We can offer the "sacrifice of praise" (Hebrews 13:15) as we join in congregational singing at church, and God will accept it and bless us. We can present our body to God as a living sacrifice and discover the will of God in fulfillment. Understanding these elements will enliven our participation in the worship services at our church. When we sing, pray, give, testify, teach, and support, we are offering a sacrifice to God just as real as those bulls and goats were that were offered by an Old Testament priest.

Remember, God does not accept every sacrifice. He rejected Cain's sacrifice (Genesis 4:2–7). He rejected the sacrifices of the people in the days of Isaiah (Isaiah 1:10–15; 66:1–4). In Proverbs 15:8 we read, "The LORD detests the sacrifice of the wicked, but the prayer of the upright pleases him." God rejected the sacrifices of the Israelites in Amos's time (Amos 5:21–23). But you, a holy and royal priest, can offer Him acceptable sacrifices. Your co-workers, family, neighbors, friends, and acquaintances may be like the people of Judah, Jerusalem, and Israel. Their prayers and offerings may be repulsive to God because they have not received Him and are living in rebellion against Him. Because God accepts your prayers, they need you to pray for them. Do you know some people who need the ministry of a God-appointed holy and royal priest? Awaken to your position and God-appointed role! Be a good steward of that responsibility.

You are to "proclaim the excellencies of Him who has called you out of darkness into His marvelous light" (1 Peter 2:9 NASB). He called you out of the darkness of lostness and sin into the marvelous light of His salvation to be an example of His excellent work.

The world does not consider Christ to be excellent. They blame Him for all the bad things that happen. They criticize Him for not making things better, not stopping wars, not ending child abuse, and allowing crime. They question the truthfulness of His Word. They have little use for the gospel of His death and Resurrection. They think being saved is strange and impractical.

Christ needs for you to show them by living a converted life that He is truly excellent. They need to know that salvation works in the daily lives of ordinary people. They need to see that Christ's salvation, truly making Jesus Lord, solves addiction problems, changes criminals to productive citizens, makes honest people out of liars and shoplifters, cleanses adulterers from guilt and sinful activity, makes people better parents, turns greedy people into giving people, and more. They need to know that personal conversion is God's solution to war, crime, and abuse. You are in a better position than even a professional priest to show the world that salvation does more than make people go to church.

Wouldn't you agree that such a priestly ministry is needed? Jesus, our great High Priest, practiced this kind of ministry. He went about doing good. He touched people where they hurt and ministered to their felt needs. And He opened the door to eternity for them. Jesus commanded us to be salt and light!

PRACTICE YOUR PRIESTHOOD.

Your employment position is an excellent place to begin. Whether you are the top executive or the least-paid employee, your priestly ministry is needed and effective. Your body is a temple of the Holy Spirit (1 Corinthians 6:19–20). Wherever you are, there is a holy temple indwelt by God. I am not suggesting you begin to conduct worship services while the boss expects you to be working. You show how excellent Christ is by your attitude toward the others who work around you.

Does the love of Christ radiate from you? Does the Fruit of the Spirit grow on the tree of your life? People are impressed with love, joy, peace, patience, kindness, goodness, faithfulness, gentleness, and self-control. When they notice, simply mention that Christ has corrected your attitude. By proving that saved people make excellent employees, you show the excellence of Christ. The Bible says we are to work as if Christ were our employer (Ephesians 6:5–7). Those are the sacrifices that shine the light of Christ into the darkness where you work.

Your family, the primary place to practice your priesthood, is also the most difficult place because your family knows the real you. No Christian is perfect. It is acceptable to be imperfect, admit you are imperfect, and continue to grow. It is not acceptable to claim perfection when everyone else knows better. Your family needs your priestly ministry of prayer, kindness, love, and attentiveness. If they are not saved, Christ will shine through you.

Saved family members need the ministry of other saved family members. Husbands and wives show Christ's excellence by loving and honoring one another (1 Peter 3:1–7). Parents show the excellence of Christ by bringing up children in the discipline and nurture of the Lord. Children minister as priests by honoring their parents. Even sibling rivalry can be overcome by the application of God's grace and acceptance. Problem-solving skills that reflect what Christ taught about confrontation, confession, and forgiveness are excellent priestly activities. Whatever your position in the family, you have a priestly role to fulfill that will minister the grace of God.

Your position in public life and citizenship calls for the practice of your priesthood. Every Christian is a citizen; some are also elected or employed public officials. Integrity, honesty, and fairness are desperately needed. We need public officials who are Christian. What a great opportunity to let Jesus shine! In our government, the officials reflect the people who elect them. America and all other nations need to turn to God and His values. Christians, leading the way, can show that Christ's salvation makes excellent citizens. When we vote, when we pay our taxes, as we drive down the road, when we are dealing with public officials, we can prove Christ is excellent by letting Him control our conduct and conversation.

When you suffer, your position is one of the best platforms for exerting your priestly influence. A sufferer is expected to be mean-tempered, dirty-tongued, and generally out of sorts. I visited the hospital room of one of our church members. She was not a happy camper. She was fussing about the nurses, the care, the food, the temperature, and everything else. When the nurse responded to her call button, I stood and listened as she verbally attacked that nurse without mercy. Then she paused and said, "By the way, I want you to meet my pastor." I did not want that nurse to know that patient was a member of my church—or any church for that matter. Her witness was completely counterproductive.

When a person who is in pain displays the spirit of Christ through their patience, compassion for others, and faith in God, the excellence of Christ's salvation shines brightly. Christ, who died on the Cross and prayed for those who nailed Him there, can give you the grace to have a sweet and gentle spirit in the midst of suffering. Such a ministry turns a hospital room into a cathedral and a bed of suffering into an eloquent pulpit. The Apostle Paul learned to glory in infirmities (2 Corinthians 12:7–10). Think about how many people have been ministered to by Job's sufferings even though he has been dead for thousands of years.

Your position with your associates, whether they are your Sunday School class, your Women on Mission® group, your neighbors, or any other group, gives you a ministry responsibility. Your place in the group may be as leader, follower, or quiet supporter. Each role is vital to the group and each position offers an opportunity to show that Christ is excellent. Letting Him control your otherwise uncontrollable tongue will exert great and positive influence. We must never be content with merely avoiding evil. We must exert a positive message of how excellent Christ is. Here is some great advice: "Do not let any unwholesome talk come out of your mouths, but only what is helpful for building others up according to their needs, that it may benefit those who listen" (Ephesians 4:29).

Even the position you have with your enemies provides a need for responsible, Christ-directed action. Your enemies may be those in faraway places, but they are more likely to be in your own household (Matthew 10:36). Jesus commanded us: "Love your enemies, bless them that curse you, do good to them that hate you, and pray for them which despitefully use you, and persecute you" (Matthew 5:44 KJV). Your enemies oppose you with hostility. To curse someone is to call for evil to befall that person. To hate someone means to maintain an attitude of hatred. To despitefully use someone means to insult, falsely accuse, threaten, treat abusively, or insult. And to persecute means to make one flee. In spite of this vile treatment, Jesus said to love our enemies with the love described in John 3:16, invoke the blessings of God on them, and pray for them, because then you act like your Heavenly Father. Jesus practiced this kind of love toward His enemies; He can enable you to do it also. At times I pray, "Lord, I cannot love and bless and pray for this person in my strength; give me your love for them." When I pray like that, I remember that Jesus suffered on that Cross for my enemies, just as surely as He suffered for me. He loves them and—with His help—I can love them.

Your church position calls for your priestly ministry. Fulfill the responsibility that Christ and your fellow Christians have placed on you. Do it with a spirit of gentleness, not manipulation or haughtiness. Follow with a gentle spirit the leadership of those who occupy the positions. Pray for one another. Let Christ purge out all selfish motives and competitiveness. "Make every effort to keep the unity of the Spirit through the bond of peace" (Ephesians 4:3). Go to church to render a ministry, and you will be ministered to abundantly (Hebrews 10:24–25). Encourage others and you will find encouragement!

Is Christ excellent to you? Show it by being a good steward of your positions.

REFLECTIONS

1. Read again 1 Peter 2:5–10, then write your own paraphrase of these verses.

2. Take time right now to prayerfully accept your priesthood from God, even though your understanding of it may be inadequate.

3. Ask God to help you learn how He wants you to practice your priesthood.

4. Write a list of ways you can practice the responsibilities of your priesthood.

CHAPTER 9

BE FAITHFUL
SHARING THE GOSPEL

Then Jesus came to them and said, "All authority in heaven and on earth has been given to me. Therefore go and make disciples of all nations, baptizing them in the name of the Father and of the Son and of the Holy Spirit, and teaching them to obey everything I have commanded you. And surely I am with you always, to the very end of the age."

—MATTHEW 28:18–20

Therefore, if anyone is in Christ, the new creation has come: The old has gone, the new is here! All this is from God, who reconciled us to himself through Christ and gave us the ministry of reconciliation: that God was reconciling the world to himself in Christ, not counting people's sins against them. And he has committed to us the message of reconciliation.

—2 CORINTHIANS 5:17–19

The Crown Jewels of the United Kingdom comprise one of the world's greatest collections of wealth. A few years ago my wife and I went to the Tower of London to see that awesome display. I never imagined precious gems existed like the ones we saw that day. Huge diamonds seemed almost alive as they radiated the colors of the rainbow. Rubies and emeralds added to their brilliance. Pearls—rare, large, unique, and abundant—glowed as if lighted from within.

Security was intense. Men, armed and alert, were stationed every few feet. The potential of theft was always on their minds. Electronic surveillance aided them in their duty of keeping that treasure safe. The line of viewers was kept moving. We were frequently reminded that taking pictures was forbidden.

The sight of so much beautiful wealth moved me deeply. I thought of the "riches of God's grace" (Ephesians 1:7). Of course, the riches of God's grace are not material things like jewels and gold. In heaven, we are told, the streets are paved with gold and the foundations garnished with precious gems. God has riches much more valuable than jewels and money!

What do you think is God's most precious possession? What is dearest to His heart? To what has God, across the eons of time, given the thoughts of His unsearchable mind? And what causes rejoicing to break out in the presence of the angels?

The answer is found in a single verse of Scripture—"For God so loved the world that he gave his one and only Son, that whoever believes in him shall not perish but have eternal life" (John 3:16). The salvation of the lost is dearest to God's heart. Before He laid the foundation of the earth, His unsearchable intelligence devised the plan for the lost to be saved (Matthew

25:34; Ephesians 1:4; Hebrews 4:3; 1 Peter 1:20; Revelation 13:8). Very dear to God's heart is His only Son. Yet He said no to the plea of His Son from Gethsemane: "My Father, if it is possible, let this cup pass from Me" (Matthew 26:39 NKJV). The Scripture says, "with God all things are possible" (19:26). Yes, it was possible to let the cup pass from His Son.

But it was not possible to both save the lost and spare His Son the death of the Cross. So God chose to save the lost! The rest of Jesus' prayer was "not as I will, but as you will" (Matthew 26:39). God's eternal will is to save the lost. The angels, who announced the birth of the Savior, "long to look into these things" (1 Peter 1:12). They ministered to Him during His temptation. More than 12 legions of angels were ready to protect Him from being crucified. Jesus said that, "there is rejoicing in the presence of the angels of God over one sinner who repents" (Luke 15:10).

God's great concern is expressed in His message through Ezekiel: "Say to them, 'As surely as I live, declares the Sovereign LORD, I take no pleasure in the death of the wicked, but rather that they turn from their ways and live'" (Ezekiel 33:11).

The gospel of salvation is the heart of God's greatest treasure. And God has trusted us with that gospel! Jesus in His life, death, and Resurrection provided the gospel. When He returned to His Father, He put the gospel into our hands. If we are not good stewards of the gospel, then His lifetime of work, His sacrifice on the Cross, and His powerful Resurrection will be for naught.

Meditate on this: if we are poor stewards of our body, we will suffer physically. If we fail in stewardship of our mind, we will suffer mentally. If we waste our talents and time, we will miss valuable opportunities. Mishandling relationships will cause us social suffering. Poor stewardship of our possessions will cause us financial problems. But if we are not good stewards of the gospel, people will miss heaven and suffer in hell forever. If we are not good stewards of the gospel, the lost cannot be saved (Acts 4:12). These statements compare the very important with the most important. *Yes, the stewardship of the gospel is by far our most important area of stewardship.*

IT WILL PAY US TO DIG DEEPER. WHAT IS THE GOSPEL?

As you probably know, the word *gospel* means "good news." The Bible tells us that Jesus went to Galilee preaching the good news of God (Mark 1:14). Peter and John preached the gospel in many Samaritan villages (Acts 8:25). And Paul wrote, "woe is me if I do not preach the gospel!" (1 Corinthians 9:16 NKJV).

What is this gospel (good news) that they preached? The essence of God's good news is in three statements recorded in 1 Corinthians 15:3–4: "Christ died for our sins . . . he was buried, that he was raised on the third day."

Christ died for our sins. Though "the wages of sin is death" (Romans 6:23), the good news is that Christ died in our place and paid the death penalty for our sins. God made that sacrifice, and it is complete payment for all our sins. Because of Jesus' death we have assurance that God forgives our sins when we confess them. Therefore, God justifies us (3:23–26). Being justified includes being declared not guilty!

Jesus really died. The Roman officer in charge, being very familiar with death, certified to Pilate that Jesus was indeed dead. "Since the children have flesh and blood, he too shared in their humanity so that by his death he might break the power of him who holds the power of death—that is, the devil—and free those who all their lives were held in slavery by their fear of death" (Hebrews 2:14–15).

When Jesus was buried, they sealed His body in a rock tomb. He was not in an intensive care unit, hooked up to life-support systems.

Jesus won the victory over our greatest enemy, death. Good news! We can face death and burial without fear. Christ has proven that burial of the body is not to be dreaded for those who commit their spirit into the hands of God. Hallelujah!

Someday, unless Christ returns first, they will lay my body in a casket, carry it out to a cemetery, and bury it six feet in the ground. If you want to shop for the abode where your body will spend the most time, shop at the mortuary. But Christ was raised from the dead! Have you let that good news sink deep into your heart? No news can be as good! During His ministry, it is recorded that Jesus exercised His power over death by restoring three people to life—the son of the widow of Nain (Luke 7:11–15), Jairus's 12-year-old daughter (Matthew 9:23–25), and Lazarus (John 11:38–44). They were brought back to life on this side of glory, but, had to die again. Jesus was raised on the other side of death, never to die again.

Jesus said, "Because I live, you also will live" (John 14:19). His Resurrection is God's promise that we shall be raised from the dead when Christ returns (1 Thessalonians 4:13–18). We will have a new and perfect body, a body like His (1 John 3:2). We will never die or suffer any kind of pain again. Forever we will worship and serve our Lord. Good news! Hope!

THE GOSPEL OF SALVATION IS FOR EVERYONE.

The gospel is for children who grow up in a Christian home. I saw a 14 year old respond to the invitation to publicly confess his faith in Christ. He grew up in a Christian home and in our church. *The gospel is for children raised in Christian homes!*

Of course, the gospel is for people who grew up in America. A few months ago, a couple in their early twenties came to my office to discuss wedding plans. I discovered the man had not trusted Jesus to save him, nor was he raised in a Christian home. He said that his sister died about a year ago, and he had been thinking a lot about God since then. When I asked if he would like for me to take the Bible and show him how to be saved, he said yes. I read Romans 3:23; 6:23; and 10:9. I told him that when he believed in his heart that Christ died for his sin and arose from the dead to be his Savior—believed this enough to make Jesus his Lord—he would be saved. Immediately he said, "I make Him my Lord." I did not even get to the part about calling on the name of the Lord. *The gospel is for people raised in America!*

The gospel is for people who have committed unspeakable crimes and wickedness. I was sitting in a visitor's cell at the county jail, talking with a teenager who had participated in a gang murder of three drunk men. I read the three verses in Romans mentioned in the previous paragraph (they are frequently called "The Roman Road"). Then we knelt and through his tears he confessed his sin to Christ, asking Him to forgive and save him. When we finished praying, while we were still on our knees, I had him read again these words: "Whoever calls on the name of the LORD shall be saved" (Romans 10:13 NKJV).

Then I asked, "Did you call on His name?" He replied, "Yes." I asked, "Did He save you?" He replied, "Yes, yes!" At that very moment the jailor opened the door and brought in his mother and dad. He jumped from his knees, hugged them, and shouted, "Jesus has just saved me!" *The gospel is for sinners!*

The gospel is for people of every race and culture. While on an evangelistic crusade in Sapporo, Japan, I noticed a beautiful young Japanese woman who responded to the invitation. In the counseling room, my interpreter told me her story. She said, "I am a stewardess for All Japan Airlines. We fly into Sapporo one day each month and spend the night here before we return to our point of origin. I saw the advertisement for the crusade at the hotel and decided to attend. Tonight you preached on a woman who had a thirst in her soul that was filled with Christ [John 4]. I have had that thirst for a long time. I have gone to the temples and left thirsty. I fly with the wealthy people and realize they have the same thirst, so it cannot be filled with riches. Tonight, when I asked Jesus to come into my soul and be my Savior, the thirst was satisfied." *The gospel is for everyone!*

Jesus commanded us to, "Go into all the world and preach the gospel to all creation" (Mark 16:15). We do not know who will receive or who will reject. We do know that everyone must hear the gospel. Our stewardship is not complete until everyone has heard. Our personal stewardship is not complete until we have done all that is possible, in the power of God's Spirit, to tell everyone. Our efforts must include telling, praying, and sending.

CHAPTER 9

WE ARE STEWARDS OF THE GOSPEL.

Christ gave us the gospel and left it up to us to declare it to everyone. What an awesome stewardship! It is awesome in its potential for great glory or great shame. Great glory involves a multitude that no man can count, from every race and nation, standing in heaven and praising God for saving them (Revelation 7:9–10). Great shame is ours if we do not proclaim the gospel to every person on earth. If we do not tell them, they will not be saved. The Bible asks "how can they believe in the one of whom they have not heard?" (Romans 10:14). Two passages in Ezekiel suggest horrible guilt if we are unfaithful (Ezekiel 3:17–21; 33:7–9).

A few years ago a mockingbird built a nest in a vine in our backyard. Because the vine is only about five feet above ground level, I could walk by and see into the nest. One day I noticed she had been sitting on four eggs. They hatched. I happened to walk by the nest while the mother was gone to find food. The tiny birds were so new they had very little shape, but one bird had its mouth open to the sky, asking for food. That day the bird could not make a sound. One day it would sing beautiful songs and soar through the air with ease, but then it was just groping for something to eat. From a distance, I watched the mother return to the nest, carrying a bit of food in her beak. Those birds would never fly or sing if she did not feed them; they would die. She fed them, they lived, and they became grown flying, singing mockingbirds.

The unsaved are like those tiny birds. They have a hunger but do not know it is for Christ. They have no idea how their lives will soar when He sets them free. They do not know the songs of glory that can fill their hearts and minds. They have no hope of heaven. They simply stand with the mouth of their soul open, waiting for some responsible gospel steward to give them the bread of life. If we fail to be good stewards of the gospel, they will never be free; they will never sing; they will perish in their sin.

If, however, we are faithful in proclaiming the gospel we will bear much good fruit. Souls will be saved forever, and we will rejoice with them in glory. Churches will be built up. Christ will be glorified. Heaven will rejoice. Family life will be improved. Children will have better parents, and parents will have better children. Our nation will be blessed. Our hearts will sing and we will hear our Lord say, "Well done, thou good and faithful steward."

REFLECTIONS

1. What is the gospel?

2. Plan specific steps you will take in becoming a better steward of the gospel.

3. Review the eight things God has entrusted us with (see chapter titles). Rewrite this list using your own words, and add additional areas if you think of them. Arrange the list in your own priority order.

CHAPTER 10

BE FAITHFUL WITH THE SECRET OF SUCCESSFUL STEWARDSHIP

I am the vine; you are the branches. If you remain in me and I in you, you will bear much fruit; apart from me you can do nothing.

—JOHN 15:5

For the Spirit God gave us does not make us timid, but gives us power, love and self-discipline.

—2 TIMOTHY 1:7

If anyone serves, they should do so with the strength God provides, so that in all things God may be praised through Jesus Christ.

—1 PETER 4:11

But we have this treasure in jars of clay to show that this all-surpassing power is from God and not from us.

—2 CORINTHIANS 4:7

an you imagine a woman, living in a rather primitive country, and married to a military man from Ohio who is stationed there? He is nearing his transfer back to the United States so he sends her to his home in Ohio while he finishes his assignment.

His house—now her house—in Ohio has carpet, something new to her. It obviously needs cleaning. She is told to use the vacuum cleaner that is in a closet. She has never seen a vacuum.

She finds a machine in the closet so she sets it on the carpet and begins pushing it back and forth. The floor is still not clean. She pushes it faster and more vigorously, but no clean floor. She spends the better part of a day doing that—with no success.

Finally, a neighbor happens by to welcome her, discovers her dilemma, and shows her how to plug the power cord into an electric outlet.

That story is so absurd it borders on insulting our intelligence. Yet many Christians are trying to be good stewards in the same way that woman was trying to vacuum the floor without power.

It took Jesus about three years to get the apostles to understand they could not serve God in their own power. He used many methods. When He sent them out to evangelize, He gave them authority to drive out evil spirits and to heal diseases (Matthew 10:1). But later He let them experience failure in their efforts to heal the demon-possessed boy. Jesus came on the scene, rebuked the demon, and the boy was cured instantly (17:14–20).

When He asked them how they would feed 5,000 hungry men with their limited lunch of only five loaves and two fish, they admitted their inability. So, in their presence, Jesus blessed the bread and fish and multiplied it to feed the entire crowd (Mark 6:32–44). Again He gave them an experience of switching from their own power to God's power, but they failed to see it.

The night before His Crucifixion, Jesus told them the secret of successful stewardship with this statement: "I am the vine; you are the branches. If you remain in me and I in you, you will bear much fruit; apart from me you can do nothing" (John 15:5). Note His statement: "apart from me you can do nothing." The word is *nothing*, not *some* things or *very little* but nothing!

In Gethsemane, Jesus commanded His disciples to watch and pray. They fell asleep because, as He told them, "The spirit is willing, but the flesh is weak" (Matthew 26:41). After His Resurrection, Jesus warned the disciples to wait until they were empowered by the Holy Spirit before going out to minister (Luke 24:49; Acts 1:8). Though He taught and trained them, they were not to try to serve Him in their own power. He would supply the power; they were to supply submission, willingness, and obedience. When they finally stopped trying to serve Christ in their own strength and submitted to God's power, they became successful, powerful, and fruitful stewards.

This is obviously a difficult lesson for all of us to learn. Paul lamented the weakness of the flesh in his letter to the Romans (Romans 7:18–19). Only Christ can give us the power to do right, to witness, or to be a good steward. In our own power we do the "works of the flesh" (Galatians 5:19–21). Only in God's power is the Fruit of the Spirit produced (vv. 22–23).

ALL POWER COMES FROM GOD.

Since the beginning God has possessed all power and the authority to exercise it. He exercised His power in creating the heavens and the earth. Since creation, He has demonstrated His power by maintaining and governing His creation. He manifested His awesome power when He raised Jesus from the dead. At the end of the age, God will manifest His power by destroying evil and by establishing complete righteousness and justice.

God has endowed His creations with limited power. For example, gravity gives power to falling rocks and atoms possess atomic power. Chemical and physical power are obvious. Some of God's creations are endowed with life and the power of procreation. Animals have muscle power. Man has amazing power: mental, physical, social, procreative. God also assigns nations the power to govern. God's gifts of power are evident all around us.

CHRIST HAS ALL POWER.

Christ displayed God's power during His lifetime, healing the sick, making the blind see, the deaf hear, the lame walk, and even restoring dead people to life. He showed power over the forces of nature when He stilled the storm on Galilee, and when He fed more than 5,000 people with five barley loaves and two fish.

Christ, in His life on earth, did His mighty works in the power of the Holy Spirit (Luke 4:1, 14). In His incarnation, Christ "emptied Himself, taking the form of a bond-servant, *and* being made in the likeness of men" (Philippians 2:7 NASB). It is easy to see that happen physically as He became a little baby in Mary's arms.

Christ chose to live by faith and according to Scripture (Luke 4:18–21; Matthew 26:54, 56). His entire life is an example of what it is like to live in the power of God.

After His death for our sins and His Resurrection by the Father, He was restored to His pre-incarnation glory. He announced, "All authority in heaven and on earth has been given to me" (Matthew 28:18). We read in Ephesians 1:20–21 that the Father "raised Christ from the dead and seated him at his right hand in the heavenly realms, far above all rule and authority, power and dominion, and every name that is invoked, not only in the present age but also in the one to come." So Christ's power is greater than all other power.

Amazing as it seems, Christ has made His power available to us. Paul discovered this, appropriated it, and said, "I can do all this through him who gives me strength" (Philippians 4:13). Paul prayed that those converted to Christ under his ministry would know by experience "the exceeding greatness of His power toward us who believe, according to the working of His mighty power" (Ephesians 1:19 NKJV).

We have the same assignment He gave the apostles. We must have the same power they needed. Can we learn what they learned—to switch from depending on our power to depending on God's power? Please do not hear me saying that we will then have a trouble-free life and religious thrills. Those apostles were not severely persecuted until they switched to God's power. Then they were put in jail, beaten, stoned, and killed. Yet, they were truly awesome, successful witnesses.

HOW DO WE MAKE THE SWITCH?

Wake up to reality. God has all power. God wants us to serve, be stewards, and work for Him in His power. Some time ago, as I planted a tree, my neighbor's three-year-old son wanted to help me shovel the dirt. His little hands closed on the handle of the shovel and refused to turn loose. He put his foot on the shovel and tried to push it into the ground, but it did not move. I put my big foot on the other side of the shovel, supplied the power, and the shovel slid deep into the ground. He tried to lift the shovel full of dirt, but again he could not move it. I let him hold on while I supplied the power to lift the dirt out of the hole. He was jubilant! He called for his mother to see the hole "he" dug. Being a grandfather at heart, I was made happy by his joy. I believe God wants to be involved in our daily lives like that. He wants to supply the power so we can be victorious in stewardship, and all of us will rejoice in the victory! Could it be that God allows us to bump up against our limited power so often because He is trying to show us we need to make the switch?

Decide to switch. Jesus called for that decision by giving His disciples commands to serve but to serve only in His power. His commands call for a decision. It is a little like switching on the light. The power company has the power ready, available, and waiting, but we must decide to flip the switch. This calls for self-denial because often we are too much like the child who says, "I want to do it by myself."

Obey His Word! The power comes when we obey and not before. When the day of Pentecost came when the harvest was ripe, when the followers of Jesus waited in obedience, prayer, and willingness to witness, then God empowered them. When Peter was on trial before the same men who had tried Jesus, he was filled with the Holy Spirit the moment he began to speak (Acts 4:5–12).

Trust God to supply the power. He told us not to worry about what to do or say when the time comes for action. He promised the Holy Spirit would supply all that we need. He is ready and waiting. Abide in Christ!

The secret of successful stewardship is found in switching from our power to God's power. Make the switch!

REFLECTIONS

1. What can you do apart from Christ? Does your life demonstrate that you believe this?

2. Describe the difference between living in human power versus living in God's power.

3. This chapter lists steps we can take to switch to God's power. List them. What steps do *you* need to take?

TEACHING SUGGESTIONS

Group study: For a two-hour study, allow an average of 15 minutes per chapter. If all participants have read the book, use the Reflections questions at the end of each chapter to guide the study. If not, use the chapter-by-chapter suggestions below.

CHAPTER 1
FOUNDATIONS OF FAITHFUL STEWARDSHIP

1. Discuss the idea of "proper management" and these three foundational truths of stewardship:
   - God owns everything.
   - God has entrusted some of His possessions to us.
   - God holds us accountable.
2. Discuss the foundational truth that God holds us accountable for what He entrusts to us.

CHAPTER 2
BE FAITHFUL WITH YOUR BODY

1. Give all participants a blank sheet of paper. Ask them to make two lists: (1) the positive features of their body and (2) their least favorite body features. Assure them that this is their personal list; they will not be asked to share it with anyone.

2. Ask people to find the seven actions (section headings) of body stewardship and list them on a chalkboard. Discuss as seems useful.

3. Discuss the similarity between the making of an Old Testament sacrifice and the presenting of your body as a living sacrifice; how Jesus used His body to glorify God; and the possibility of today's Christians glorifying God in their bodies through death.

CHAPTER 3
BE FAITHFUL WITH YOUR MIND

1. Discuss the characteristics of the natural mind. Ask participants to suggest examples of these characteristics.

2. Lead the group to form a definition or description of the spiritual mind.

3. Help the group identify our responsibilities for renewing our minds.

CHAPTER 4
BE FAITHFUL WITH YOUR ABILITIES

1. Ask the group to help you make two lists: (1) common abilities with which a Christian can glorify God and (2) uncommon abilities with which a Christian can glorify God.

2. Ask half the participants to read Romans 12:6–9, 1 Corinthians 12:8–10, and Ephesians 4:11 and identify body gifts mentioned. Ask the others to compose a list of gifts needed in your church.

3. Ask participants to discuss reasons why the lists (from question 2) are not exactly the same.

CHAPTER 5
BE FAITHFUL WITH YOUR TIME

1. Ask: Do we all have the same amount of time?
2. Discuss the meaning of "redeeming" time (Ephesians 5:16).
3. Discuss why establishing good priorities and setting healthy boundaries are essential to good stewardship of time.

CHAPTER 6
BE FAITHFUL IN YOUR RELATIONSHIPS

1. Write *Our Cultural Heritage, Our National Heritage, Our Family Heritage,* and *Our Spiritual Heritage* on posters. Ask participants to suggest ways we can be stewards of each of these.
2. Ask participants to list the relationships in their lives (children, spouse, church, friends, etcetera). Again, ask participants to suggest ways we can be good stewards of these relationships.

CHAPTER 7
BE FAITHFUL WITH YOUR SUBSTANCE

1. Define *substance* as it relates to our study.
2. Ask someone to be prepared to share a testimony of their stewardship pilgrimage regarding their substance. Allow others to share if they wish.
3. Lead the group to discuss these questions: (1) why should we honor God with our substance and (2) how can we honor God with our substance?

CHAPTER 8
BE FAITHFUL IN YOUR POSITIONS

1. As someone reads aloud 1 Peter 1:1–10, ask members to listen for ways God qualifies every believer to be a priest.
2. Provide enough copies of recent newspapers for each member of the group to have a front page section. Ask them to locate an article in which someone needs the ministry of a Christian priest. Ask each one to share briefly their article and describe how a 1 Peter 2 priest would minister in that situation.

CHAPTER 9
BE FAITHFUL SHARING THE GOSPEL

1. Help the group understand the word *gospel*. Define the word, focusing on the description given in 1 Corinthians 15:1–4.
2. Ask: If we honestly accept our responsibility as trusted stewards of the gospel, how does it change our lives?

CHAPTER 10
BE FAITHFUL WITH THE SECRET OF SUCCESSFUL STEWARDSHIP

1. Ask: Can we be successful stewards without the power of Christ? After discussion, ask someone to read John 15:5.
2. Ask: What do we learn when we fail because we do not depend on God's power?
3. Close the study in prayer.

SCRIPTURE INDEX

CHAPTER 1
FOUNDATIONS OF FAITHFUL STEWARDSHIP

- Don't forget the Lord • Deuteronomy 8:11–14
- Everything belongs to God • Psalm 24:1–2
- Gifts and ministries God gives • 1 Corinthians 12:4–7 NASB
- Sermon on the Mount • Matthew 5:1–7:27
- Lord's Prayer • Matthew 6:9–15 NASB
- Rest for your soul • Matthew 11:28–30 NASB
- Two most important commandments • Matthew 22:37–40
- Parable of a faithful servant • Matthew 25:14–30
- Summary of Christian life (Great Commission) •
  Matthew 28:19–20
- House (like faith) built on a rock • Luke 6:47–48 NASB
- Guided by the Spirit • John 16:12–13 NASB

CHAPTER 2
BE FAITHFUL WITH YOUR BODY

- Sex outside marriage • Exodus 20:14; Leviticus 18:22–23;
  1 Corinthians 6:15–18
- None are good • Psalm 14:2–3 NASB
- Fearfully and wonderfully made • Psalm 139:13–14
- Body thrown into hell • Matthew 5:29
- All have sinned • Romans 3:23

CHAPTER 3
BE FAITHFUL WITH YOUR MIND

CHAPTER 4
BE FAITHFUL WITH YOUR ABILITIES

- Tabernacle artisans gifted by God • Exodus 31:2–6
- David relied on God • 1 Samuel 17:33, 37
- God trains us for our battles • Psalm 144:1
- Use your abilities with all your might • Ecclesiastes 9:10
- Jesus is fed by the Father's will • John 4:31–34
- Apart from Christ we can do nothing • John 15:5
- Dorcas's gifts lead to many believing in the Lord • Acts 9:36–42
- God gives everything • Acts 17:25
- Differing gifts but the same Spirit • 1 Corinthians 12:4–11, 14
- Paul's "Thorn in the Flesh" • 2 Corinthians 12:7

CHAPTER 5
BE FAITHFUL WITH YOUR TIME

- Wait for the Lord • Psalm 37:7
- Number your days • Psalm 90:12
- Time for everything • Ecclesiastes 3:1–8
- Sheep among wolves • Matthew 10:16 NASB
- Not my will • Luke 22:42 NKJV
- Christ didn't seek His own will • John 5:30 NKJV
- Christ finished the work • John 17:4 NKJV, John 19:30
- Will of God • Romans 8:27; 13:6–8; Galatians 1:4; Ephesians 5:21–33; 6:1–4, 6; Philippians 2:13; 1 Thessalonians 4:3; 5:16–18; 1 Timothy 5:8; 1 Peter 2:13–15; 3:17; 4:19
- Becoming like Christ • Romans 8:29
- Clothe yourselves with Christ • Romans 13:12–14

- Jesus destroyed the power of death • Hebrews 2:14–15
- Longings of the angels • 1 Peter 1:12

CHAPTER 10
BE FAITHFUL WITH THE SECRET OF SUCCESSFUL STEWARDSHIP

- Flesh is weak • Matthew 26:41
- All authority given to Christ • Matthew 28:18; Ephesians 1:20–21
- Without Jesus we can do nothing • John 15:5
- Treasure in jars of clay • 2 Corinthians 4:7
- Weakness of the flesh • Galatians 5:19–21
- Fruit of the Spirit • Galatians 5:22–23
- Working of His power • Ephesians 1:19 NKJV
- Strength through Christ • Philippians 4:13
- Spirit of power, love, and self-discipline • 2 Timothy 1:7
- Serve with God's strength • 1 Peter 4:11

New Hope® Publishers is a division of WMU®, an international
organization that challenges Christian believers to understand and be
radically involved in God's mission. For more information about WMU,
go to wmu.com. More information about New Hope books may be
found at NewHopePublishers.com. New Hope books may be
purchased at your local bookstore.

Use the QR reader on your
smartphone to visit us online at
NewHopePublishers.com

If you've been blessed by this book, we would like to hear your story.
The publisher and author welcome your comments and
suggestions at: newhopereader@wmu.org.

Business as
Missions in Action

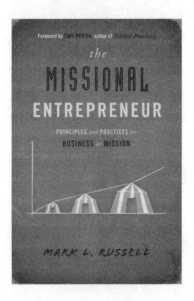

The Missional Entrepreneur:
Principles and Practices for Business as Mission
978-1-59669-278-7 • $24.99

For information about our books and authors,
visit NewHopePublishers.com.